NO WAY BABY!

Exploring, Understanding and Defending
the Decision Not to Have Children

KAREN FOSTER

ISBN: 1439268568
ISBN-13: 9781439268568

I am called the Virgin Queen.
Unmarried, I have no master.
Childless, I am mother to my people.
God give me strength to bear this mighty burden.
—Queen Elizabeth I

But I Want Grandchildren! 141

Who Will Take Care of You When You're Old? 153

You'll Regret It! 175

Epilogue: Now What?
Finding Your Childfree Purpose. 191

Introduction

What to Expect When You're Not Expecting...

I am at a party talking to a very nice woman I have just been introduced to when suddenly she asks me the fatal question, "Do you have any children?" I ponder my options. Do I answer with a plain and simple "No," or go with the other reply, "No, I chose not to have children?" I know from experience that both options have their own risks and predictable results. I decide to go with the simple "No" and it brings the conversation to a screeching halt. I can see it in her eyes: she is plagued with concern and indecision about where to go next. She is asking herself what this could mean. *Has she just not had them yet? Looks like she may be getting too old. Is she one of those anti-kid people? Don't want to go there. Is she infertile? Maybe it's a touchy subject. Better abort (pun intended)!* Next will come an awkward pause followed by an abrupt subject change. "Oh…so what type of work do you do?" or "Where are you from?" I know what to expect; I've been here before.

I want to relieve the strain, so as I watch her puzzling through the options, I interject with the second response, just under the buzzer. "No, I chose not to have kids." At this point, my fellow partygoer raises her eyebrows as if I've just admitted to being a space alien. Sounding surprised, she says, "*Really*?" This is immediately followed by an endless sermon about how great her kids are, how she couldn't imagine her life without them, how she loves being a mom and all the drawn-out reasons why. Who's she trying to convince?

This is the point when I usually want to shout at the top of my lungs, "Listen, this choice of mine is not an attack on your own, so don't take it personally!" But instead, I plunge into a sermon of my own about how yes, kids are wonderful, and I just love and adore my nieces and nephews, and how some of us are natural-born aunties while others are natural-born mothers, and on and on and on.

Perhaps you can relate?

Openly admitting you don't want to have children puts some parents instantly on the defensive. Declaring you are childless by choice—or, more succinctly, childfree—can leave you open to a whole slew of objections from friends, family, and even complete strangers. You are capable of having children, and still you have chosen not to? You must be a selfish, career-obsessed hedonist. Certainly no one will ever want to marry you. You are depriving your spouse of children and your parents of grandchildren. You are not contributing to the next generation and will be a burden to society in old age. You are foolish and will certainly live to regret it.

Sound familiar?

When will it stop? Isn't the right to make our own choices in life regarding marriage, family, and career what our mothers and grandmothers demanded for us? The many paths available to women today, of which motherhood is but one, are the direct result of a long social battle fought over many decades. From suffrage to the women's movement, those who came before us put everything on the line so we could have fuller, richer lives.

Think about it: as little as fifty years ago, the idea that childbearing could be a choice was nothing less than absurd. As a woman, if you didn't have children you were labeled a "spinster" or "barren," both social kisses of death that resulted in a fair amount of whispering. As a man, your choices were also slim. Given the social pressures of the day, you were unlikely to find a woman who didn't want to have children. Your choices were either never to marry or to marry and have children you didn't want. Well, at least you got to stay at work all day.

It is no wonder we are far from perfecting our conversation on this topic. We easily forget that parenting as a choice, not an obligation, is an extremely new concept. To put the childfree option into play, certain social changes had to take place, the most essential being unrestricted access to effective birth control. Although the American Birth Control League (later Planned Parenthood) was established in 1921, the dissemination of birth control literature by mail (the primary means of communication at the time) was classified by federal law as obscene until 1936. (1) As we all know, however, just because something is made law doesn't mean society is ready to accept it. Throughout the 1940s and 1950s, birth control advocates were still engaged in numerous lawsuits and legal battles. It wasn't until 1965 that the last U.S. law prohibiting the use of birth control among *married* couples was finally struck down (2), and not until 1972 that the Supreme Court ruled that the right to privacy also protected an *unmarried* person's right to use birth control. (3) I was four years old then. So, if you find the subject awkward, difficult, or even risky, remember that as far as social change goes, it is in its infancy (but growing fast!).

Of the sixty million women between the ages of fifteen and forty-five living in the U.S., 42 percent do not have biological children. (4) That's about twenty-five million women. Some will have children one day, others will raise stepchildren and/or adopted kids and so on, but approximately 6.2 percent of all women will make the conscious choice to remain childfree, up from 4.9 percent in 1982. (5) I wonder what would happen to that number if having children was seen as a choice rather than an expectation. What if it was actually debated along with our other major decisions, such as where to go to school, what career to choose, where to live, whom to date, whether or not to marry, and so on?

According to the latest research, 50 percent of pregnancies each year are unplanned. (6) "Unplanned" doesn't always mean "unwanted" or even "unwelcome," but in a supposedly enlightened society that's a lot of oopsies! The rate of unplanned pregnancies tells us that a massive number of adults are giving little thought to one of the most life-altering decisions they will ever make.

Individual change takes time, and social change takes even longer. In the past, there was probably some comfort in the clearly defined roles of men and women, but there was serious discomfort as well. The women's movement of the late sixties and early seventies didn't come out of nowhere. For women to revolt in such numbers, the level of dissatisfaction had to run very deep. The result was a rejection of narrowly defined roles and the lack of status that went along with them. The new opportunities that opened up to women as a result of the movement were revolutionary, and we continue to climb to new heights, as evidenced by our 2008 presidential election. The one downside to the women's movement was that it left some women feeling demeaned in their roles as wives and/or mothers. Fortunately, that transgression is being corrected with the return of the stay-at-home mom in all her glory. The rift is not completely healed between the career mom and stay-at-home mom, as evidenced by the many books and articles written about the so-called "mommy wars." However, the unspoken resentments and judgments between parents and childfrees are not even spoken about, much less given a catchy title.

Rather than pitting our choices against each other, why not acknowledge what a coup it is to even have a choice? In many parts of the world, women (and men, for that matter) don't have a choice about where to live, whom to marry, what type of work to do, and, least of all, whether or not to have children. I feel fortunate to live in a place where both the subject of this book and writing it are my choices to make. Whether we contribute our energy to creating children or to other creative endeavors, we are all working toward a better, brighter future.

That is why I want to clarify a point right up front. This book is not an attack on those who choose to have children. Nor is it the spearheading of a movement or a recommendation to abstain from reproduction. However, even after decades of revolutionary social change, those who choose to remain childfree continue to fall victim to a multitude of faulty assumptions and ridiculous objections. Many of these objections are overt and calculated attacks. Others are more subtle refutations. Some of these condemnations mask the unfortunate regret of a reluctant parent. Frequently, they stem from a lack of understanding as to why we would choose to go without something that others simply can't imagine doing without. I hope this book will help build greater understanding in four ways.

First, if you are still exploring the decision of whether or not to have children, then in these pages you will find a rare opportunity to research the childfree option. There is certainly no shortage of information about becoming a parent, but very little about not becoming one. If, after weighing your options, you choose to have children, you will have made a conscious, thoughtful decision, and I commend you. Of course, if you choose not to have children, then welcome to the club.

Second, if you have already chosen a childfree life, congratulations. Here is your guide for dealing with *la résistance*. Together we will debunk the most common myths about the childfree, whether they linger in your own mind or are perpetuated by those around you. With this book in hand, you are armed with all of the information you'll need to quell fears and counter skepticism. Whether you're dealing with a parent nagging about grandkids or a friend filling you with fear about being old and alone, you will never be at a loss for words while standing your ground.

Third, if you are childless by circumstance—be it infertility, health limitations, or just never having found the right situation to start a family—you will find in these pages a new perspective on life. It is my hope that this book will help you make peace with the choice chance and/or happenstance has made for you. I applaud your willingness to turn child*less* into child*free* by exploring these pages.

Finally, if you are a parent, relative, or friend of a childfree adult and you just don't get it, this book will answer your questions and abate your fears. The paths of parent and non-parent alike have many joys, sorrows, expectations, and dreams. Although we are on different roads, each is connected to, and ultimately part of the unifying human experience. I hope this book will put your mind at ease and help you understand and accept your childfree loved one's decision.

In the following pages you will read a combined response to the most common assumptions made about the childfree. I have intertwined the insights of fifty other childfree adults from the U.S. and Canada with extensive research supporting their arguments and, of course, my own two cents. Because the decision to have children or not has more of an impact on the lives of women, much of our discussion will be from the female perspective. However, I have included comments from several insightful childfree men as well.

A while ago, I told a friend of mine about my plans to interview fifty childfrees for my book. "Really? You are actually finding people to interview?" she said, thus revealing her assumption that I was an anomaly at best. Yet, after placing only a few postings on various websites around the country, I was inundated with replies from childfree adults who were eager to tell their stories. Hearing their experiences in such depth was both an honor and a privilege. I found myself making friends all over the nation, from Portland, Oregon, to Detroit, Michigan, to New York City. I found that there are as many reasons for not having kids as there are child-frees, yet similar assumptions are made about all of us. Ignored by politicians, policymakers, and so on, I heard how invisible many childfree adults feel in a society that claims to put families first, regardless of the reality on the ground. I learned that while many childfrees have a tough time with family and friends, some just breeze through with almost no resistance. I was also happy to hear the assuredness and peace of mind overwhelmingly exhibited by those I talked to. The childfree life may evoke criticism from some, but the benefits to those who choose it far outweigh any sticks and stones.

While I offered the use of a pseudonym to everyone I interviewed, only two took me up on it. The childfree can take the heat or they wouldn't be living the lives they've chosen. The quotes I have included are in the subjects' own words, except where edited for readability and flow. Not all childfrees share the same social and political views, and not everyone will agree with every argument presented in this book. I have provided various arguments in support of the childfree life; I encourage you to take what you like and leave the rest for others.

I use the term child*free* for two reasons: first, because typing "childless by choice" over and over was just too laborious; and second, because it distinguishes those of us who are intentionally forgoing parenthood from the child*less*, who may not be that way by choice. So let's go ahead and see what, as a community, we have to say for ourselves to those who continue to thwart us. Do their objections hold water once they are thoroughly examined? You decide.

1
So, You Don't Like Kids?

Now the thing about having a baby—and I can't be the first person to have noticed this—is that thereafter you have it.
—Jean Kerr

All too often the assumption is made that those who choose to live childless by choice, otherwise known as childfree, just plain don't like kids. This may be true for you, but even if you like children or even adore children, you are asking yourself if the idealized version of family bliss portrayed on television and in movies is really attainable. You may have looked at the pros and cons, thought about your own dreams and desires, and been honest with yourself about whether or not parenting is the right choice for you—not an easy task in a culture that commonly doesn't even talk about parenthood as a choice. When was the last time you heard someone say to a young person "if you have kids" rather than "when you have kids"?

In a society that values freedom of choice and rugged individualism, certain assumptions continue to be made about how life should go. With the stagnation of the women's movement and the chokehold of religious and social conservatism experienced over the last three decades, it has been harder than ever to follow your dreams if they take you in a direction other than the expected one. Perhaps that chokehold will loosen a bit with a relatively new administration in Washington. However, even as we enter a new, more progressive era, it is hard to ignore the fact that President Obama's fabulous wife and two adorable daughters play right into the conventional wisdom of what makes an ideal family.

With the persistent depiction of marriage and family as the pinnacle of social success, the childfree can end up questioning themselves with the same protests others throw at them: *What is the matter with me? Am I selfish? What about relationships and/or marriage? What will happen to me when I get old? Will I regret it?* It is human to want to belong, which makes the temptation to deny our true feelings and go along with the crowd very strong indeed.

The invisibility of the childfree in popular culture doesn't help. We are living in one of the most pro-natal periods in recent history. Everywhere we look; it seems the "baby rabies" epidemic is growing exponentially. Baby rabies are defined by urbandictionary.com as "the lapse of sanity in which a person feels that s/he absolutely MUST have a baby in the very near future, and will often go to great lengths to get pregnant and will bitch constantly about wanting a baby in the meantime. Usually happens in women, but men get it occasionally, as well." In my experience, baby rabies also signifies a demarcation point at which the psychological need for a baby exceeds the biological need, becoming a relentless obsession. A glance at the surface of American life would certainly indicate that the condition is contagious and spreading.

The many industries involved in the creation, care, feeding, and entertainment of new life rake in billions of dollars each year. Politicians, conservative and liberal alike, speak ad nauseam about protecting children and families, at least during their campaigns. To attract new employees, companies boast of their family-friendly policies and develop their benefits packages accordingly. Countless parenting books and magazines offer the latest and greatest techniques for raising happy, well-adjusted children. As a result, parents have an endless supply of resources at their disposal for blissful family life—don't they?

On the surface, it sure looks like we live in a child-loving society. So what's wrong with us, the childfree? Why don't we want to jump on the baby rabies bandwagon? Is it that we dislike children, or is there something else going on beneath the surface—a deep, dark secret that hides the truth of how parents and children are really benefiting, or not benefiting, from the marketing machines and political promises that are supposed to create strong families? If it's all so fantastic, why are many parents and kids stressed, vulnerable, or even out of control?

FREE-RANGE CHILDREN

We see them at the mall, in movie theaters, on the airplane, and even in our own neighborhoods: misbehaving, rambunctious children screeching, squealing, and running amok. "Where are their parents?" we lament. "Is it me, or are kids today completely out of control?"

Like me, you have probably noticed that the grocery store is a sort of social biosphere displaying current parenting styles, and worthy of scientific study. While every parent must occasionally deal with the public embarrassment of a tired and cranky child acting out, scenes like this one, which I witnessed while writing this book, seem to be increasingly common.

While doing a little shopping I came upon a mother with her seven- or eight-year-old son. I could tell the young boy was whining about being told no to something he wanted; common and normal enough. I was feeling my usual sympathy for this poor mom when suddenly the boy blurted out, "You're an asshole, Mom!" The mother, perhaps out of embarrassment, just brushed off the offense and kept walking while her son followed behind, stomping his feet and hollering further obscenities. After what seemed like an eternity, but was probably just thirty seconds or so, the mother turned around, exasperated, grabbed a box of sugared cereal and tossed it into the cart, thus ending the spectacle for the moment.

After I picked my jaw up off the floor, three thoughts came to me. First, if I had pulled something like that as a kid, the half-full shopping cart would have been left right there in the aisle and my mother would have dragged me home, where my troubles would be only beginning. Second, what kind of stress must that parent be under not to have the luxury of ditching the cart and doing some hands-on parenting? Finally, the third thought was that perhaps spectacles such as this, which seem to be more and more common, play at least some role in the decision not to have children.

Sure enough, as I talked to more and more child-frees, this type of scene was often complained about—but it wasn't the children they blamed; it was the parents.

Lisa is a twenty-six-year-old Canadian nursing student living in Portland. *"A lot of people seem to let their children just run around wild, and the parents are oblivious. They're not paying attention because they're so used to tuning them out or they don't care. That really gets to me. I grew up to believe there are certain things you just don't do in public. My mother was very strict, so when I was growing up and you went out in public, you behaved and that was it. But it's not like that anymore."*

Sandi is a forty-eight-year-old professional who is also disturbed by lackadaisical parenting styles and their results. *"I sound like my mother talking about how 'kids are these days,' but if I had done half the stuff I see kids getting away with I would not be alive now. My mother and my father would have killed me. I was taught to respect people, to say please and thank you, and I just don't see that stuff as often anymore."*

Instead, what we see are television shows like ABC's "Nanny 911" or "Supernanny," which are excellent reminders of just how out of control unsupervised and overindulged children can become. Each week, stressed-out parents are called on the carpet for their lazy, permissive parenting and the resultant monsters they are now struggling with. Actually, these shows are a great source of affirmation for the childfree life! They are also a reminder that parenting actually takes work, dedication, and commitment, and that raising a functioning human being means interacting, setting limits, and sometimes being the bad guy.

Another reality show that took on the difficulties of parenting was NBC's "The Baby Borrowers," which aired in the summer of 2008. This social experiment took teenage couples who were anxious to start their adult lives and gave them a chance to see firsthand what parenting was all about. The couples were given a house and a baby, followed by a toddler, a young child, a teenager, and finally a senior citizen. Then, in true reality-TV fashion, their many fights and meltdowns were broadcast for our amusement.

While this was the first piece of popular culture I'd seen to demonstrate a more realistic view of parenthood, there was a fair amount of controversy over the judgment of parents who would lend their babies and toddlers to teenagers, and the parents of said teenagers who offered up their teens for national ridicule. "In an increasingly frivolous nation, we have now turned caring for our children and our aged parents into a game, and their suffering when the care falters into entertainment. How lovely," (1) wrote Robert Bianco of *USA Today*. The ads trumpeted, "It's not reality television, it's birth control!" However, serious ethical questions were raised about the safety and well-being of all the children involved, including the teenage "parents." In fact, the American Academy of Child and Adolescent Psychiatry (AACAP), a professional medical group representing the majority of child and adolescent psychiatrists in America, called on NBC to pull the plug on this social experiment, citing serious trauma to infants and toddlers who were separated from their real parents for days at a time.

After airing the show in 2008, NBC prepared and broadcast a special episode, "The Baby Borrowers 'Town Hall Meeting,'" to address the issues about the show and its lasting effects. All of the teenage "parents" had since broken up and gone their separate ways, and all had decided not to have kids anytime soon. While the risks to the participants were too great for NBC to move forward on a second season of this reality show, the true reality is that if all aspiring parents had an opportunity to safely participate in such an experiment, the number of unintended pregnancies and unprepared parents would surely diminish.

It is astonishing to learn that in the United States, 50 percent of pregnancies are unplanned. (2) It stands to reason, then, that many new parents are completely unprepared and ill-equipped for the very difficult job of raising a well-adjusted member of society. No wonder so many parents seem to take the path of least resistance, whether it is ending a scene over sugared cereal by giving in, flipping on the TV just to keep them quiet, or doing whatever else it takes to satisfy the whims of their children so they won't make a fuss. The result is something one teacher I spoke with can attest to, because she deals with the offspring of bad, or perhaps overwhelmed, parents every day.

Page, forty-four, teaches middle school math. *"As an adult working with kids, I see every day the importance of learning simple things like 'no means no.' Not 'no, and we'll talk about it later' or 'no, until I change my mind,' but just 'no.' I feel like some kids learn the meaning of 'no' for the first time from me. I shock them because I am the first adult who ever said it and meant it. Whether in a classroom, out in public, or in a family unit, you just can't do whatever you want whenever you feel like it."* She goes on to say, *"The interesting thing about being a teacher and being childfree is that I have a 'get in free' card with parents that gives me some credibility. While I try very hard not to give parenting advice to others, I brought up the importance of 'no' to some friends at dinner and I was never so sorry in my whole life. The husband attacked the wife, saying, 'See, I told you,' and suddenly I was in the middle of an argument that I didn't even know they were having. At the same time, their kid is just terrible. He acts up and he manipu-*

lates the mom, and she just won't step up. But if a two-year-old always gets his way, how are you going to keep him from getting his way when he is ten or fifteen? What about when he is an adult? How often as an adult do we fully get our way? How will he deal with that?"

If you feel like more and more parents have simply become subservient to their children, you are not alone. It is unrealistic to think that, as a childfree, you will never have to endure a weeping toddler on an airplane or unruly children running wild on a subway. A certain amount of that is normal and unavoidable. Intolerance for scenes like the one I described in the grocery store, though, doesn't make one anti-child or coldly lacking compassion for the stress parents endure. In fact, it turns out that you don't even have to be child-free to find these scenes deplorable, whether they are on reality TV or are just plain reality.

In an article for *Newsweek*, Carrie Friedman explains how she truly wants to have kids, but the unruly children left to run amok in fancy restaurants, R-rated movies, and other adult venues make her question herself. That, on top of the relentless pressure to join the exclusive "parent club," is enough to turn her off to the whole prospect completely. In Friedman's article, she recounts the agony of sharing an exciting work accomplishment with a friend, only to be told she would never know real happiness until she has a baby! (3)

Yet, if having children is the pinnacle of true happiness, then it stands to reason that there would be lots of research to support this. Not true. Study after study shows how marital and/or life satisfaction actually decreases when children come on the scene, often rebounding after the birdies leave the nest. "Despite what we read in the popular press, the only known symptom of 'empty nest syndrome' is increased smiling," (4) writes Daniel Gilbert in his book, *Stumbling on Happiness*. To support this statement, Gilbert cites four different research studies, all of which show that early marital satisfaction decreases with the arrival of the first child and does not fully rebound until the last child leaves home.

The most recent and thorough piece of research on parenting and life satisfaction comes from Robin Simon of Florida State University and Ranae J. Evenson of Vanderbilt University. In 2005, their combined research concluded that no group of parents—be they parents of babies, toddlers, or teens, or even if they are empty nesters—report less depression than those who have never had children. (5) This seems a little counterintuitive in a society that describes a newborn as "a bundle of joy"!

Why, then, does the conventional wisdom that children are the undisputed bringers of happiness prevail? The answer, says Gilbert, is that "the belief-transmission network of which we are a part cannot operate without a continuously replenished supply of people to do the transmitting, thus the belief that children are a source of happiness becomes a part of our cultural wisdom simply because the opposite belief unravels the fabric of any society that holds it." (6) More simply put, if word got out, we could be in trouble as a species.

There was a time when people were eager to have many children because they were needed for labor, plain and simple. But in the information age, children have moved from the asset column to the liability column. Instead of having lots of children to work on the farm, parents have very few children and live in servitude to them. Thus, *wanting* children becomes more and more essential to human survival, and the belief that everyone *should have* children persists. It is from this place that the myth of motherhood as the undisputed fulfillment of a woman is born. Living in contradiction to this is seen, perhaps unconsciously, as a threat to our very existence, giving rise to the notion that the childfree must be some sort of coldhearted monsters. Something must be wrong with us, because otherwise the prevailing wisdom begins to crack and crumble. Yet not wanting children means only that we have stepped outside that belief-transmission network, taken off the rose-colored glasses, and made a decision based on the realities of parenting, not an idealized vision swirling around the collective imagination. Unfortunately, it is the idealized vision that draws many grownups in, and perhaps is to blame for the subsequent disillusionment that results in stressed-out parents throwing up their hands, turning on the TV babysitter, and serving choco-sugar-crunch every morning in an effort to avoid an ugly scene that was not part of the vision.

With the lack of real support for parents and children in our dog-eat-dog, hypercompetitive culture, it's no wonder that parents are stressed and angry. While the rest of the industrialized world has embraced ideas such as lengthy paid maternity leave, paternity leave, subsidized childcare, universal healthcare, forty-hour workweeks, and generous vacation time, here in America the burden is fully on parents, which may come as a surprise to some once the initial fawning from friends and family over that first child has ended. Parents and children suffer as a result, as do the rest of us who have to live with the unsupervised and undisciplined generations to come.

Jennifer M. is a thirty-six-year-old retired U.S. military teacher living in Germany. *"When I see other Americans out in public with their poorly behaving children, I'm ashamed to be an American in a foreign county. German kids are seldom seen or heard, and parents would never dream of taking them everywhere they go. Their little economy cars have no room for this anyway. Seldom do I see a badly behaved German child in public!"*

NO KIDS ALLOWED

Another reason German children may be rarely seen in public is because with a birthrate of 1.37 (7), there aren't many (more on that in chapter 3). But here in the U.S. there is a very different attitude about when it is appropriate to include children and when it is not. The mere mention that there are places people shouldn't bring their children puts a lot of parents on the defensive. Maybe this is because they resent having to choose between fine dining and family-friendly dining. Perhaps they want to pretend that, even though they have had a child, nothing has changed; they've given up nothing. It is possible that strong maternal instincts elicit protectiveness when mothers feel that their kids are unwelcome or unwanted. One could speculate even further, but no matter what their reasons, you may be surprised by the irrational behavior of even the most otherwise rational people when you try to exclude their offspring from an obviously adult venue.

Cindy, a forty-year-old designer, loves children, which is why she was shocked by the resentment she experienced the one time she held an adult-only event. *"I had a big fortieth birthday party at a really great teahouse. I had it catered and everything; it was my big hurrah and I did it all myself. I had friends from all walks of life there, about one hundred and twenty-five people in all. On the e-vite I had written, 'Adults only, please.' Before the party, I heard through the grapevine that one of my friends had received the invitation and taken it completely personally. She has a one-year-old daughter, and for some reason she thought I was speaking just to her, as if at forty years old I would have only one friend with kids! She argued that because it was at a teahouse she should be able to bring her daughter. Another friend tried to convince me to give in, saying we could just pass her around and it wouldn't be any big deal. But it was a big deal! It was an adult event with drinking and so on. There are appropriate times to have children somewhere and times not to. Just because it was called a teahouse didn't mean it wasn't a bar-like setting. There was no place for kids there. Yet another friend chimed in and suggested that if the parents weren't going to come as a result, why not just let them bring her? Of course, if I had let one bring kids, I would have had to let everyone. Besides, the point was not to exclude this one set of parents. It wasn't about that. I wanted to have an adult cocktail party! I felt so terrible and so guilty. The parents did not respond to the e-vite and did not show up to the party. We still haven't really talked since then. But I realized that I shouldn't be the one feeling bad. I have lots of friends who have kids and they didn't have a problem with it. Why should I be made out to be the bad guy when I just wanted to have a grown-up party on my fortieth birthday?"*

Meagn is a forty-nine-year-old data coordinator whose rather strict rules about children in her home have been met with a fair amount of criticism. *"While my friends all know and accept me just as I am, I have run into people I barely know that find out I don't permit small children in my house and tell me I must be a horrible, empty, bitter person to have a rule like that. But I did that because it's not a place you can run around unsupervised. I have a lot of breakable things; it's not baby-proofed in any way; and these days a lot of people raise their children in what I like to call 'free-range' style."*

Excluding children is a risky business, a Brooklyn branch of Barnes & Noble discovered in 2006 when it banned strollers from its lower level. Although the store had created a parking area for the baby buggies, there was no appeasing the irate parents of the Park Slope neighborhood who were crying foul. According to the bulk of the ensuing online debate, lots of parents and nannies were using the local B&N as an adjunct day-care center. But regardless of the tattered and torn books strewn across the children's section, or the blocking of grown-up sections by hordes of unattended strollers, parents seemed to think the mere request that they show some common courtesy was an attack on their offspring by the child-hating public. Perhaps posts like this one spurred that belief:

"Yes, there are plenty of self-centered childless people walking around. WALKING. Not rolling their offspring in a gigantic plastic tub thingy and announcing their reproductive ability (like it's something unique) by making a big, loud, tacky fuss about every little thing their kid does or doesn't do/know/say/eat. It's just invasive. That's why there's so much hostility. Stop invading our lives with yours."

But the majority of the comments seemed to be searching for some common ground while keeping the blame where it belonged.

*"I guess they [*B&N*] had to make a judgment whether they would lose more sales from people being frustrated that a stroller was blocking an aisle or from making it more difficult for people*

without children to browse the store. Personally, I'll withstand a little inconvenience that a stroller in my way causes in exchange for children getting to hang out in a bookstore, no matter what my opinion of their parents may be."

Underlying this debate was a question of whether or not we as a culture feel that parents or non-parents should ultimately have the right of way. The real issue, though, was the level of courtesy shown by both, and the sense of entitlement each so vehemently accused the other of exhibiting. One online comment summed it up quite nicely: *"Whether an asshole does or does not have children is irrelevant to their status as an asshole."* Amen to that. In the end, parental entitlement won and Barnes & Noble revamped its approach with a sign "suggesting" that parents park their strollers rather than requiring it. Just a few accusations of discrimination against children and *voila!* the de facto day care reopened.

Limiting access or excluding children altogether from your event, home, or business may have unpleasant consequences. Yet childfrees and even some parents out there would agree that whether you want to have an adult-only event like Cindy, or you have more sweeping boundaries like Meagn, or you are simply trying to protect your business interests like Barnes & Noble, the exclusion of children from inappropriate venues is hardly an anti-child stance. In fact, it may be for their own good. Nicole, a childfree friend of Cindy's and an interviewee we will hear from later, attended the adult-only fortieth birthday party and shared that it was really wild (and fun!), but that no responsible parents would have wanted their children there. How can kids learn to respect limits if their parents don't recognize them? And as Meagn pointed out, it can be dangerous for kids whose parents don't teach them good boundaries. She is within her rights not to take on the liability for that in her home. Furthermore, in New York, where small stores are crammed with gobs of people, is it so much to ask that parents exhibit a little common courtesy, not just to the other customers but to the business itself? After all, Barnes & Noble provides a free play area for kids that can be used without obligation of purchase and a special parking area for strollers. It seems that the least parents could do is meet the store halfway.

THE GOOD, THE BAD, AND THE UGLY

To be fair, indulgent, entitled parents raising wild children is not the whole picture. There are lots of parents out there who really do the work of parenting and are raising well-adjusted kids; we just don't notice them so much because they aren't making a big fuss everywhere they go. Many childfrees have a friend or family member who is blessed with one of those "easy" babies that makes them double-check their own decision to be childfree. Of course, the true childfrees still come back to their original conclusion, which demonstrates a well-thought-out, mature choice. Summing up how the entire childfree population feels about children in general, though, can't be done. There are varying attitudes among us that are sometimes black and white, but more often are shades of gray depending on the child, the parents, the ages, and so forth.

Most childfrees I spoke to either like kids or are neutral toward them. But yes, there's also a portion of childfrees who honestly dislike children, and some who are even willing to admit it. *"I like kids fine, so long as they're cooked properly,"* joked one childfree. Publicly admitting you don't want to have children can be difficult enough, but to admit you don't like them takes the social risk to an even deeper level. Lori, a forty-three-year-old parale-gal, found out firsthand the dangers of admitting she was less than enamored with kids when she made her feelings on the subject clear during a national television interview.

"This was my fault," she self-incriminates. *"I was work-ing at a big law firm of about a hundred people when I did a 20/20 interview about being childfree. Well, after that I was called every name in the book. I was called 'monster' and 'evil'; it got really nasty. My secretary stopped talking to me. She said, 'I didn't realize you hated working mothers so much!' even though I hadn't said anything about working mothers on the show. Finally, the tension got so bad that I was called into the head of litigation's office. He was somewhat understand-ing of my situation, but there was nothing I could do. I wasn't going to change just to make those people happy. It wasn't like I was running around with an 'I hate kids' T-shirt or had anti-kid stuff up around my office."* So what was the offend-ing statement that got Lori's secretary and other co-workers in such a tizzy? When probed about the accu-sation that childfrees are selfish, Lori pointed out that parents wanting to replicate themselves are also selfish. She may have been protected by the First Amendment, but that did little to protect her against the marginaliza-tion and personal attacks she experienced from her co-workers after the fact.

Disliking children or just preferring adult settings is not a crime. However, if you have an aversion to chil-dren, you probably don't need to be reminded that, just as there are adult settings where children don't belong, there are family-friendly settings where they do. Some childfrees I talked to shared various ways to minimize interactions with kids, other than throwing an "adult-only" party or visiting bars every weekend. One woman asks to be moved in restaurants so as not to be seated near kids; others stay away from "family-friendly" social engagements; and still others avoid cultivating friend-ships or romances with parents whenever possible. Children can't really help it if parents drag them along to inappropriate adult venues. Luckily, as a childfree adult, you often get to choose whether or not the activi-ties, events, and social engagements you participate in include children. And, while the parents are stuck at Chuck E. Cheese (or the kids' section of Barnes & Noble), you get to dine in peace and quiet. Not a bad deal, eh?

In contrast, many childfrees I spoke with really like or even love children. Some had preferences toward cer-tain ages, preferring babies or big kids or teens. While I am impressed by the honesty of childfrees who admit they don't really like kids, personally I am somewhere between the "like" and "love" categories, depending on the kid. But it hasn't always been that way. There was a time when I really didn't like children at all and made no apologies for it. Frankly, I didn't have to; I come from a small nuclear family, and there just weren't many little children around as I grew up. None of my friends married or had children young, so I wasn't exposed to kids that way, either. Back in my twenties, I felt awkward when I did come in contact with children, not knowing what to say or how to interact. It wasn't until I was thirty years old that the first of my friends had a baby, and that little girl was the first infant I ever held. Eventually others started jumping on the baby train, and then along came my first niece, whom I instantly fell madly in love with. Even when she was colicky and refused to be comforted, I was undeterred. Now when someone hears I am childfree and says "but it's different when you have your own," I have some idea of what he or she means. Still, even the arrival of my second niece, who melted my heart as quickly as her big sister had, didn't change how I felt about having my own. Then came my adorable nephew, who can't seem to go anywhere without drawing a crowd—but now I am sounding like a bragging parent.

If as a childfree, you dare to demonstrate your love for children, then you may have heard comments resembling this: "You're so good with kids! Too bad you're not having any; you'd be a great mother." But being a great auntie is different from being a great mother. No matter how much energy we put into playing with someone else's offspring, we still get to give them back once the kids get cranky—or once we do. Still, those of us that are great with kids but don't want to have our own perplex our parenting peers, leading them to ask: "If you like kids so much, why don't you have some?" What these objectors don't realize is that we might be great parents, or we might not, but after examining the reality of parenting and how that would impact our other hopes and dreams, we realized it just wasn't the right choice for us.

Elisabeth is a PhD-level psychologist who specializes in child and family therapy. *Because I got into social services my mom sees all my compassion and empathy and she tells me I would be a great mom. She thinks it's too bad I won't have kids because she sees my potential there. But fortunately, she agrees that if I don't want them I shouldn't have them."*

A lot of thought goes into the decision to be child-free. If more adults reflected on whether or not to have children rather than just falling into the assumption of parenthood, we would have far fewer unwanted children and lots more cool aunties and uncles. There are plenty of perks to being the "cool auntie," and if you are a childfree who loves kids, you are worth your weight in gold to your friends and family who have young children.

Vince and Nicole have been together for fifteen years and never wanted children, but they're an asset to their parenting family members. *"We both always thought that if we really wanted children in our lives there are other ways to do it. We love being the cool aunt and uncle. My sister has two kids and we hang for the weekend, spoil them rotten, and then give them back. It's great for us, the kids, and my sister."*

Janet, forty-four, is a marketing manager for a large tech company. *"I have taught my friends' kids to sew, to bead, to cook, and all sorts of things like an aunt might. Since most people don't live around extended family anymore, I fill that role for them."*

It really does take a village to raise a child, and like Vince, Nicole, and Janet, many of the childfree villagers provide much-needed support. In the days of the isolated nuclear family, having a childfree sibling or close friend who enjoys children means babysitting options, weekend retreats, and other help that just wouldn't be available otherwise. It's one of the many ways that we childfrees contribute to the next generation.

In fact, while writing this chapter I was watching my best friend's daughter play with her toys on the floor of my office. I have found myself providing lots of support to her and her mom, who are like family to me. Unfortunately, a few months after the birth of her daughter, the father became controlling and threatening. Fortunately, she had far more resources available to her than so many women in that situation do, and after a particularly frightening encounter with the dad, she took her daughter and left. During the months that followed there were many times when she needed support with her growing daughter and rambunctious dog. Even though I live about three hours away, I was only too happy to oblige. I often dropped everything to either take them in to my little home or travel to where she was and provide the help she needed. As honorary auntie, I was able to pull babysitting duty so Mom could get some business done, meet with her lawyer, or even take a much-needed break and get a massage. I know that meant a lot to her, as it did to me.

The reality is that, had I been bogged down with a family of my own, I just wouldn't have been able to offer the help and refuge that I did. I can't imagine having to sit by and watch all that she went through without being able to lift some small piece of the burden. It struck me as incredibly ironic that even while I was writing a book on being childfree, I was contributing to the wellbeing of a child. I plan to continue supporting my dear friend, a newly single mother, in any way I can.

Other childfrees also have been able to answer the call from families in crisis. Louise is a thirty-nine-year-old speech therapist. She and her husband have been a beacon of stability for their nephew, whose own family is falling apart. *"I have always been really good with kids and enjoy having them in my life. We have numerous nieces and nephews, but I have one nephew I'm very close to. My sister, his mother, is living what my own mother lived, struggling single motherhood. Recently she had to have hip replacement surgery, and she is so emotionally unstable that between the meds and the stress, she ended up angry, paranoid, and lashing out at all of us. Twice now I have flown halfway across the country to help her and my nephew. He is really hurting with his mom being that way. He asked me once why I don't have kids, and I explained all my reasons to him. He decided that we have a pretty nice life as is. Then he said, 'Well, aren't I sort of like your son anyway?' That made me feel really good, because especially with all that's happened lately, he really is."*

There is really no way to sum up how the childfree feel about children, because the range is broad and the opinions are varied. If you spent the day reviewing the many Web sites, blogs, and online bulletin boards on this topic, you would perhaps come to the conclusion that the childfree really don't like children. However, you also would be hearing only from childfrees who actively sought community. With at least five million self-proclaimed childfree women and perhaps the same number of childfree men roaming around the United States of America, the childfrees who do not seek this type of community are missing from the conversation. Logic dictates that childfrees who dislike children and/or their parents are more likely to express it online, where they are safer from repercussions. Further, a childfree who enjoys kids is far less likely to feel the need to rant about it online—or anywhere else, for that matter. There are many who don't even know there is such a thing as the "childfree" label (myself included, before writing this book). It is likely that childless-by-choice adults who don't seek out community are more supported by friends and family or are fonder of children.

I found the interviewees for this book through online communities as well as by referrals from friends and family. The referrals represented childfrees who were not affiliated with any formal childfree community. Still, until more research has been done on this growing population, generalizations are hard to make. One thing, however, is certain: The idea that all childfrees are child-hating, bitter heathens spitting in the face of the "family values" crowd is utterly false.

VALUE OF WHICH FAMILIES?

In our culture there's a lot of talk about the importance of family values. Everywhere we look, another preacher or politico begs us to "think of the children." However, living in a child-centered society does not necessarily mean we live in a child-loving society, no matter what rhetoric is spewed our way. Certainly, there is a lot of focus in the public arena on children, all designed to put a family-friendly face on policy. But underneath the rhetoric, we find that many of our policies fall far short of providing adequate support for children and families.

It has been said that the individual is intelligent but the masses are stupid. I think a similar analogy could be made about our attitudes toward children. Individually, we value the welfare of our own children, but collectively, not so much. Everything from deadly food allergies to lead-tainted Chinese toys to toxic baby bottles made with bisphenol A (BPA) has struck fear and panic into the hearts of parents, and *poof!*, like magic, public policy has been born in the name of children. On the surface, this would seem to indicate a society dedicated to the well-being of kids. Sadly, though, the threats to children that get action versus those that are ignored say more about the values of society than any sermon or political speech.

Food allergies, especially in children, who are understandably careless when away from home, are really scary for parents. In November 2005, the media went wild with the so-called "kiss of death" that killed a fifteen-year-old Canadian girl whose reported peanut allergy was triggered after kissing her peanut-butter-munching boyfriend. (8) The ensuing headlines were alarming, stirring the fear embers and pulling on our heartstrings. However, the coroner's report later showed that the victim had actually succumbed to a severe asthma attack that cut off the oxygen supply to her brain. (9) The stories correcting the sensationalism of the initial reports were buried in the back of newspapers, if reported at all, thus perpetuating the myth of a widespread peanut butter danger. But how widespread is this threat, really?

In the article "Peanut Allergies and School Bans on Peanut Products: Sound Public Policy or Hysteria?" (10), Carol Bengle Gilbert does the math for us. Consider that there are approximately fifty-three million children who attend public schools in the United States. Next, understand that officially approximately 100–150 people of all ages die each year from severe food allergies. But let's go ahead and make the huge leap that all 150 of these deaths happen to school-age children. That would put the total number of schoolchildren affected at .0002 percent. Yet peanut-free zones, peanut bans, and lunchbox searches are popping up like flies. Speaking of flies, according to Gilbert's article, forty to one hundred people die each year from allergic reactions to insect stings. Shall we eradicate all stinging insects from the planet? And while we're at it, over seven thousand children die each year in auto accidents. Perhaps, then, we should ban children from riding in cars. No? Well, this clearly demonstrates that those rallying us to the causes of children are often just the loudest, most fearful, or most politically astute. These well-meaning and impassioned champions of our youth often steer big chunks of resources away from the many and toward the few. For example, in 2003, an elementary school in Walnut Creek, California, hired a registered nurse to monitor the lunchboxes of an entire class in which one child was allergic. To pay for it, they had to release an instructional assistant who had served the entire class. (11) It is hard to imagine that the only way to ensure the safety of one child was to diminish the quality of education for the whole class.

Another uproar disguised as protection for children was the Chinese tainted toy scandal of 2007. Oh, what a sad Christmas it would be without any painted toys for the girls and boys. Beginning in midsummer, every time I turned on the news yet another cheap piece of junk imported from the People's Republic of China was being recalled due to the presence of lead paint. According to Nancy A. Nord, acting chairwoman of the Consumer Products Safety Commission (CPSC), "Ensuring that Chinese-made toys are safe for U.S. consumers is one of my highest priorities and is the subject of vital talks currently in place between CPSC and the Chinese government." Great. So, just how many children were reported sick, injured, or dead due to this lead-paint scourge? Zero. Okay, so that doesn't mean we should stand by while children gnaw on poisonous paint. However, the hype about lead paint largely overshadowed the fact that if industry had not exported every manufacturing job under the sun to China in the first place, we wouldn't have had this problem. Instead, we would have had lead-free toys made in America by parents with family-wage, benefited jobs. The parents affected by outsourcing probably couldn't afford too many painted Christmas toys that year anyway, but we'll all be paying for the CPSC's budget increases secured as a result of this new threat.

Then there's the hype about an alleged poison called bisphenol A (BPA), which apparently seeps out of plastic baby bottles and has been blamed for development and reproductive problems and other maladies, including cancer, diabetes, obesity and attention-deficit disorder. While the FDA still approves the chemical, an independent research firm found flaws with its study and the agency is now undertaking additional research. Numerous stores have removed these bottles from their shelves, and businesses are looking to safer replacements for BPA in their manufacturing. While we wait for the final word, it makes sense that manufacturers, retailers, and parents eschew BPA-laden products. It would be foolish to confuse a lack of definitive research with a guarantee of safety. Canada has already gone ahead with a full ban, and in the U.S. legislation to do the same was introduced in March 2009. (12) On the surface, it again looks like we are taking care of children, and even erring on the side of caution, right?

However, while the media, legislators, and parents with the time and energy to make a fuss create policy to protect their dear children from possible threats, millions of children suffer verifiable and well-documented injuries every day and we do nothing. What child-loving society would allow the following:

- Thirteen million children in America are hungry right now, this minute. (13)
- Almost 40 percent of our kids live in poverty or low-income households. (14)
- Roughly 9.4 million of our kids are without health insurance. (15)
- The United States ranks nineteenth in infant mortality. A baby born in Cuba has a better chance of survival than one born in America. (16)
- The 30 percent dropout rate has remained constant during the last two decades of supposed education reform. (17)

The number of children suffering in this rich nation cannot be denied, no matter how hard one tries. As our politicians wave the "family-friendly" flag and religious pundits speak of traditional family values, millions of kids are ignored, pushed aside, and even blamed for the sorry state they are in.

One such child was Graeme Frost, a twelve-year-old boy recovering from a very serious car accident. He explained in a radio address that if it hadn't been for the SCHIP program, he might never have recovered. SCHIP, which stands for State Children's Health Insurance Plan, covers the kids of working parents who are uninsured but not poor enough for Medicaid. His plea to then-President George W. Bush was that he sign a bill that had sailed through the House and Senate, reauthorizing SCHIP for the seven million kids currently enrolled and expanding coverage to an additional four million at a cost of thirty-five billion dollars over five years, which Bush promptly vetoed. The additional cost for the program would have been funded by a tax increase on cigarettes of sixty-one cents per pack, so depending on where you fall on the political spectrum, there's plenty of fodder here for debate. But on the family values crowd's watch, instead of real debate we got the "swift-boating" of a twelve-year-old boy and his family. The attacks came from the right, and they were relentless.

Outright lies about Graeme and his family were smeared all over the media. Some of the more tempered allegations accused him of being a rich kid coddled by the government, living in a big house and going to a private school. But the vile threats popping up on the Internet were far more hateful. The family's home address was posted online, they received calls harassing them every day, and one anonymous blogger even suggested a public hanging of the entire family.

The reality was that the big, expensive house the Frosts lived in was actually purchased in 1991 for $55,000, when the neighborhood was not so safe. The housing boom, coupled with the sweat equity Graeme's father put into the property, meant that the family had a decent place to live. As for private school, Graeme was there on a scholarship, and his sister's private school was state-funded due to the brain injuries she suffered in the same car crash as her brother. The whole point of the SCHIP program is to help families just like Graeme's avoid financial ruin in the wake of a catastrophic health crisis. Of the wealthy industrial nations, only in America would a family have to lose everything they have worked so hard for before receiving any public assistance. Our current healthcare system makes paupers of countless families and individuals, and it is a rude awakening to learn that many of us are actually one illness away from ruin.

Some voices chastised the Frosts for investing in their property rather than private health insurance. This criticism assumes that some sort of affordable private health insurance policy for a family of four exists. It doesn't. (Healthcare reform had been passed at time of publishing but its impact won't be known for some time.) As a self-employed, single, childfree person, I have personally been *denied* health insurance at any price due to a mildly degenerated disc in my lower spine. What I had considered a minor nuisance became a huge problem when I tried to insure myself. Unfortunately, it is not until this reality hits home that the blinders come off for most of us.

The stark reality we are all dealing with, whether we have kids or not, is that unpaid medical bills are the number-one cause of bankruptcy in the United States, accounting for over half the filings every year. (18) Of the estimated two million Americans affected by medical bankruptcy, seven hundred thousand are children. (19) It is even more unsettling to learn that 75 percent of those who go bankrupt under the "best healthcare system on the planet" have insurance at the onset of illness. (20) In 2005, the Senate passed a bill making it harder for working families to file for bankruptcy, while carefully preserving loopholes for the wealthy. The fallout of this legislation and its effect on families remains to be seen, but you don't have to be an economics expert to know it certainly will have a devastating impact on sick adults and children.

Whatever your position on the current state of health care in America, when you look at the vicious attacks on the Frost family, you have to ask: what pro-child society would stand for this? While we frantically set up policies to ban peanut butter and lead paint, the mandate to ensure that the fundamental needs of children—food, clothing, shelter, basic health care, and decent education—are met continues to be nonexistent. The mask of family-friendly America covers up a whole pile of apathy when it comes to the kids who are really in need. Instead, we turn our attention to hype and fear-mongering that result in public policies designed to appease some very vocal parents and allow politicians to claim they are protecting kids.

While politicians on both sides of the aisle pretend to be protecting the children, the greatest disservice to the next generation comes in the form of a thirty-seven-thousand-dollar credit card bill presented at birth. (By the way, in the time it took me to write this book I had to adjust that number up by eight thousand dollars, and once the current recession ends, who knows what it might be.) That's right; due to the $11,400,000,000,000 national debt, (21) all 306 million American men, women, children, and even newborns (22) are over thirty-seven thousand dollars in hock, and rising. Years of failed fiscal policies, including an absence of sensible regulation that brought our economy to its knees, an unnecessary and poorly executed preemptive war in Iraq, and unchecked healthcare costs are burying us in both personal and public debt. Whether or not President Obama is able to clean up a mess that took decades to make remains to be seen; however, when I see a baby I can't help but wonder what kind of start we are giving him or her. It seems to me that a little lead paint is the least of their worries.

Holly, a forty-four-year-old small business owner, observed, *"Baby boomers have gotten all the benefits from the prosperous post-Depression and World War II era, the GI Bill, cheap housing, good schools, affordable college, etc. They got all those things that their parents didn't have, but now their children aren't going to have any of that stuff either."*

The age of upward mobility and each generation outdoing the one before may be over. Numerous studies have shown that our current crop of young people is starting out in a financial hole that many never recover from. According to the Student Monitor 2008 recruitment study, the average school debt for a college grad today is twenty-three thousand dollars. A 2004 Nellie Mae survey, employing the most recent data available, adds to that an additional $2,169 in credit card debt. With the end of family-wage jobs in manufacturing and industry, college has become a luxury-priced necessity. Combine that with the absence of affordable housing, flat or declining wages, puny or nonexistent benefits, and the fact that seven out of ten low- to middle-income households report using credit cards to pay basic living expenses is easily understood. (23) Young people today face an increasingly demanding workplace that leaves little time or money to pursue any dreams, including caring for a family.

ON-THE-JOB COMPLAINING

It seems to me that if on the whole society valued children above all else, parents would insist on spending some time with them, but today's work habits tell a different story. Here in the U.S. we have had a long tradition of taking pride in our work, and many still believe that hard work will get you ahead. As it turns out, though, the thing most rewarded in today's workplace is long work, not hard work. Up until recently we talked about the long hours Americans worked, second only to the Japanese. Not to be outdone, we explained away their industriousness by pointing out how they ignored their families and committed suicide at an alarming rate. However, compared to the United States, the Japanese could now be considered a nation of slackers, and Americans have gained the title of the longest-working people in the industrialized world.

In October 2007, "60 Minutes" aired a story about just this phenomenon. The forty-hour workweek has gone the way of the dinosaurs, being replaced by a sixty- to eighty-hour workweek. In fact, Americans work longer hours and take fewer vacations than citizens of any comparable nation, including Japan. Today, the rigid, overworked ways of the East aren't talked about so much. Instead Americans hop on the "crackberry" before getting out of bed and don't stop until the wee hours of the night. Workaholism is one of the few "isms" that is actually rewarded in our culture, making it very hard to combat. When workers get kudos on Monday morning for the e-mail they sent at nine-thirty Sunday night, fifteen-hour days become what's expected.

How can Mom and Dad be good parents when they have to work all the time just to keep up? This situation has obvious consequences for families and kids due to the unavailability of parents who work under this type of pressure. However, if this long work paid off in dividends such as greater security for the family or a stronger economy and nation, it would at least have some value. The truth is far from it. It turns out that while we thumb our noses at the French with their thirty-seven-hour workweek and minimum four weeks of vacation, hour for hour they still beat us in productivity, as do several other European nations with far more family-friendly policies, both written and unwritten. Parents cannot claim the moral high ground of family values and spend eighty hours a week at the office. The two don't mesh.

So, if the culture of sixty- to eighty-hour workweeks is becoming the norm, and the family isn't benefiting, who is? Here's a hint: "If I can pay one person to do the job of two, I win. Who am I?" In the "60 Minutes" piece, Lesley Stahl interviewed two men, both dads, who left their high-pressure, six-day-a-week jobs in New York so they could spend more time with their families. Now they share one job as legal counsel to an athletic shoe company. Sounds good, doesn't it? Job sharing is one of the progressive policies employers are beginning to offer, right? In this case, however, both men are actually paid 75 percent of a full-time salary. This is because when all is said and done, both men work forty hours a week. Hmm…so they work forty hours a week but are paid 75 percent of a full-time salary? Sure works out well for the company.

Ironically, the corporate machines that have created this long-working culture tend to fall in line with that "family values" party on the right. Meanwhile, the heroes who risked everything to head the labor movement of the early twentieth century turn over in their graves. Facing financial ruin, ridicule, and even physical assault, these brave men and women picketed, held strikes, and even rioted for working conditions that honored the individual and the family. Success was theirs in 1938 when Franklin D. Roosevelt signed the Fair Labor Standards Act (FLSA) into law. Nowadays, all executives, administrative staff, computer specialists, professionals, and outside salespeople are exempt from its mandatory overtime provisions, basically rendering any job likely to come with a family wage vulnerable to the exploitation of businesses that care more about bottom lines than family time.

Yet there's more to the story when it comes to work. Whether or not one is willing to commit sixty to eighty hours a week to a job may have more to do with personality and values than with whether or not one is a parent. In the current standard of long work hours, many childfrees see their status as a benefit. They are able to take advantage of opportunities that parents in their offices can't. For others, the assumption that just because they are childfree means that they can pick up the slack for their parenting coworkers, who take advantage of their kids as an excuse to leave work early or leave tasks undone, leads to anger and resentment.

Lisa B. is a thirty-five-year-old human resources benefits specialist who appreciates the advantage her childfree status affords her. *In the workplace I have always made my childfree status common knowledge. That way no one ever worries that I'll be the one who's out with kids. I don't want them to think they can't give me a job because they assume even though I'm not pregnant now, I probably will be at some point. Even though it's not legal to discriminate that way, I think it happens anyway. Since I'm not having kids, I use that to my advantage. I want my boss to know I'm not going to come in his office and tell him I'm going on maternity leave.*

Some childfrees see advantages and disadvantages to being an unencumbered employee. *"I've traveled around the world. I have stayed in India for periods of time for my job. I have gotten some pretty plum assignments because of my flexibility and willingness to go anywhere, so in that respect it's been wonderful,"* says Vicki, forty-six, a buyer for the automotive industry. She goes on to say, *"But it's a two-pronged issue. When people have to leave the office to pick up kids, or take more sick days or what have you, I end up getting dumped on. Frankly, I'm in the midst of that right now with a woman who just found out that she's pregnant and very high risk. So I get my share of extra work because I don't have the demands on my time that parents do."*

Vicki is not the only one who feels taken advantage of, either. Many of my interviewees complained of not being afforded the same courtesy their parenting peers are when it comes to benefits, time off, and workload.

"Parents in the workplace get away with murder. They call and say they're working from home because the kids are out of school, but if their kids are home they're not getting a full day of work in. I have never seen anyone work from home with kids there and actually accomplish anything. Suggesting that people deal with family business outside of work time is unheard of, yet if I need to take time off to go out to the barn and wait for the vet to see my horse, it is not seen as a valid reason to be away from the office. On top of that, people with kids get all kinds of perks. They get company-sponsored insurance for their kids or scholarship programs, while people without kids are supposed to just put up and shut up," laments Meagn, a forty-nine-year-old data coordinator.

Kathy is fifty-one and has a master's degree in counseling. *"I resent the way companies deal with benefits and whatnot. That's one thing I really don't like. Our company will pay a portion of family insurance and then recently announced they were looking to do a scholarship fund. I can't take advantage of any of that. I wish they had an à la carte benefits program instead, where people could pick and choose. Then those without kids could take more vacation days instead of having health insurance for a child. Something like that would be fairer."*

Elisabeth, thirty, a child and family therapist, sees both sides and adds, "*Some childfree people think that just because they don't have kids they should have all the exact same benefits as parents, and I'm not sure that's true. If you have a family to support you may need some more resources, and I don't begrudge people maternity leave and things like that. But you do run into situations where people have to leave work earlier because the kids are getting home from school, or they want more vacation time, and the employees that don't have kids end up picking up the slack. Obviously, parents have to be home with their kids when they're sick, but the assumption that you should just get more vacation days, more time off, or do less work because you chose to have a family is unfair. People should weigh their commitment to work with their commitment to family and make decisions based on what they're expected to do and whether they can handle it.*"

While parents may get preferential treatment in some workplaces, for the majority of those trying to balance work and family the options for them are extremely limited. Very few companies offer such options as job sharing, flextime, or part-time schedules that would prevent the kind of limit pushing some parenting workers engage in, and the subsequent button pushing the childfree endure. Corporate life overall remains rigid, with its one-size-fits-all staffing model that leaves very little room for a life outside of work, parent or not.

When it comes to family values in America, it seems the perceived reality and the true reality miss their connection over and over again. After closer scrutiny of the so-called family-friendly face of America, it is impossible to conclude that it is the childfree who are anti-children. The truth is that society's alleged child-centricity is an act, covering up the overwhelming indifference society has to the real needs of children. It is hard to say that those of us who intentionally forgo parenthood in a family-unfriendly society are the ones who dislike children.

As a childfree person, whether you love kids, loathe kids, or are somewhere in the middle, you recognize that the last thing this world needs is another ignored child. For that reason alone, you should feel good about your decision not to bring one into the world, and so should the people around you. Instead, as all too many of us can attest to, we field accusations of selfishness and find ourselves defending a decision that ought to be venerated. So let's see how well that accusation holds up.

2
Why Are You So Selfish?

A red rose is not selfish because it wants to be a red rose. It would be horribly selfish if it wanted all the other flowers in the garden to be both red and roses.

—Oscar Wilde

Stand back; no pushing; the line forms to the right. There are plenty of accusations of selfishness and declarations of self-sacrifice to go around. The routine goes something like this:

"You don't want to have kids? What are you, selfish or something?"

"Me, selfish? You are the one desperate to replicate yourself! How selfish is that?"

"I am contributing to society through all the sacrifices I make as a parent. If everyone were like you, the human race would die out!"

"What do you mean? I'm the one making a sacrifice. If everyone were like you, polluting humans would overrun the planet and we would still die out! I'm saving the planet by not bringing another greedy consumer into the world!"

"If you really cared about the next generation, you'd make sure there was one by having children. All you want to do is stay out late, sleep in, travel, and pursue your career."

"You breeders are lucky I care about my career. Who do you think picks up the slack when little Susie has a soccer game or a case of the sniffles and you take off?"

"Yeah, but when you are old you will be a burden on society because there's no one to take care of you!"

"So you're having children just so there is someone to take care of you when you get old? That's totally selfish!"

"Well, you are depriving your husband of children and your parents of grandchildren. I would never do that. I am committed to seeing my family continue, no matter what it takes!"

"But there are so many unwanted children in the world, and yet you will spend thousands of dollars using up precious medical resources just so you can have one that looks like you!"

And so on and so forth.

No one likes being told that he or she is selfish, but the accusations of selfishness hurled at childfrees are particularly frustrating because we do not yet have our rightful place at the social negotiating table. As Lori, in the last chapter, found out, speaking up for yourself as a childfree person can elicit powerful backlash from the parenting majority. If you don't want to have kids, does it really mean that you are unwilling to give up sleeping in, relaxing weekends, nights out on the town, free time, traveling, career goals, etc.? Well, truthfully, many of us are unwilling to give up those things! But as Ellie, a thirty-eight-year-old business development specialist, pointed out, *"If coming to terms with the fact that I would not be a good mother and acting accordingly makes me selfish, then I'll take it. I am selfish."*

CUTS BOTH WAYS

Relishing the spoils of a childfree life may seem selfish to some, but the spoils do have their price. Our challenges go far beyond being relegated to the couch at holiday gatherings or being left out of "Mommy and me" conversations with friends. The exalted status of parenthood makes any complaint filed by a childfree regarding unequal treatment in our families, in our work, and even under our laws akin to blasphemy. In a society shrouded in pro-child sentiments (at least publicly, as we saw in the last chapter), many childfrees live "closeted" lives, allowing others to come to their own conclusions as to why they don't have children. Sandi is a forty-eight-year-old procurement analyst who confesses, *"When people used to ask me why I don't have kids, I often would say I couldn't have them. It shut them right up. I shouldn't have to explain myself anyway, but too many people think there's something wrong with being childfree, so I just make them feel bad for asking in the first place by saying I can't."*

Given the fact that parents are rarely asked to defend their reasons for wanting children, feeling that you must constantly defend your decision not to can be extremely frustrating. Michael, a sixty-one-year-old Macintosh computer specialist, bats back the selfishness accusation. *"Actually, people who have kids are being selfish. If you ask the reason why people want kids, it's always about themselves. I want someone to love; I want someone to love me; I want this; I want that. They are the selfish ones because they are doing it for their own selfish reasons. Very rarely do you find anyone who knows the only legitimate and good reason to do it; that's a confirmed desire to create and guide a functioning human being to live in our society."* He's got a solution. *"I would like to see a lock/unlock birth control technology developed so that at a certain age everyone would be rendered sterile. Then the only people having kids would be those who went through the trouble of taking a reversal drug. Instead, I see these overindulging, beaming idiots who let their 'shrieklings' go around invading everyone else's lives."*

You need a license to drive a car, carry a gun, and catch a fish, but anyone can have a baby, regardless of an ability to care for it. Requiring parents to demonstrate their fitness for the job before procreating sounds like a good idea, until you think about the questions of who decides which people are fit, based on what criteria, and how it would be enforced.

Similar experiments have already been conducted in the U.S. In the first three decades of the twentieth century, sixty thousand Americans were forcibly sterilized for being feebleminded, insane, epileptic, inebriated, diseased, blind, deaf, deformed, dependent, homeless, criminals, ne'er-do-wells, tramps, and paupers. (1) But the science behind all of this, eugenics, was a racist pseudo-science supported by the white upper class. The idea was that social deviance was inherited and could be eliminated by selective breeding. There was no examination of society's role in social deviation or the fact that many successful people came from adverse backgrounds. Worst of all, the eugenics laws of the Nazi Party were modeled after American laws already in place in several states, and led to the sterilization of three hundred fifty thousand Germans as only one part of Hitler's quest for a master race. While American eugenics fell out of favor after World War II, the practice continued in mental hospitals until the mid-1970s. (2)

Wanting to ensure that the next generation is healthy and well cared for is the motivation behind most suggestions that parents be required to obtain some sort of license to have children, but the idea of putting this into practice in a free society is unrealistic. We will have to find other ways to care for the neglected dependents of irresponsible parents through better education, healthcare, and opportunities. However, continuing to publicly question the motives of potential parents may be the best way to get young people to ask themselves why they want children. Ultimately, having children ensures a next generation, but as Michael so colorfully points out, when you ask around it is generally not a parent's main motivation. It stands to reason that diminishing the next generation is not the main reason for choosing to be childfree, either.

When it comes to selfishness, a better argument is that both parents and non-parents are selfish, pursuing those things that they envision making them happiest—be it having children or not. Sweeping generalizations of the motives on either side are ill-advised but the idea that childfrees have cornered the market on selfishness while parents are self-sacrificing saints is just plain absurd. Shannon, a thirty-five-year-old paralegal, agrees. *"I would have to say that everyone is selfish, whether they're childfree or not. I have had conversations with people who said they had children so they'd have someone to take care of them when they got old, or to have someone to love and love them back unconditionally, and to me those are selfish reasons to choose to bring another person into this world. So I think every person is selfish in some ways, but because being childfree is so different it is easier to label us that way."*

Another group easy to label as selfish are potential parents who ignore nature, undergo painful medical procedures, and spend tens of thousands of dollars trying to get pregnant. While some may glorify the physical and financial costs endured by these dedicated and determined parents-to-be, it is pretty obvious that the desire to replicate their own DNA has usurped the actual desire to parent.

Infertility is big business, with close to 483 fertility clinics in the U.S. collectively boasting annual revenues well over three billion dollars. (3) This has led to pain and heartbreak for many who believe that with enough time and money, fertility treatment will eventually result in a baby. The reality is quite the contrary.

According to the Centers for Disease Control and Prevention, in 2006 there were 138,198 cycles of assisted reproductive technology (ART) performed in the United States. ART is defined as any procedure that involves surgically removing eggs from a woman's ovaries, combining them with sperm in the laboratory, and returning them to the woman's body or donating them to another woman. Of the ART cycles performed, 41,343 resulted in live births—less than a 30 percent success rate. (4)

There are also ethical decisions that must be considered when pursuing fertility treatments. Many people are unaware of the waste involved in common procedures such as in vitro fertilization (IVF). In this procedure, approximately twenty-four ova are extracted from the female and then fertilized with her partner's sperm. Next, two to four of the healthiest-looking embryos are implanted in the womb, leaving the rest to be discarded in some manner. Depending on an individual's beliefs about when personhood begins, this can present an ethical dilemma. Many pro-lifers believe the soul is present at conception and see fertility clinics as committing mass murder. It is curious, then, why we have yet to see scores of weeping pro-lifers blocking the entrances to fertility clinics the way they do abortion clinics. Perhaps because when it is their turn to face infertility, or the inability to create another human to worship their version of God, they want to have some options? Maybe it is because unlike abortion, infertility is extremely profitable and there is no way a capitalistic health-care system would stand for it? Possibly it is because in a child-centric society, collateral damage in the creation of life is tolerable? Whatever their reasons, their absence from the entry doors continues to illustrate their hypocrisy. Nothing new from religious zealots, but more on that in the next chapter.

IVF leftovers are also at the crux of the ethical debate surrounding stem-cell research. Stem cells are master cells that can morph into any cell type in the body. Stem cells have demonstrated great potential in the quests to cure spinal cord injuries and diseases such as Alzheimer's and Parkinson's. However, to harvest stem cells, the frozen embryo has to be destroyed— thus the controversy. Yet it is estimated that hundreds of thousands of embryos have been destroyed since IVF began in 1978, and only the tiniest fraction have ever been available for use in medical research. Under former President Bush, the Christian right fought and won this argument for eight long years, setting potentially lifesaving research back a full decade. Fortunately, on March 9, 2009, President Obama signed an executive order ending his predecessor's ban on federal funding for this important research. But there are still legal hurdles. As a result of President Obama's executive order, scientists can do research only on existing lines of stem cells. Other legislation passed by Congress still prohibits federally funded scientists from creating new stem cell lines. Many research advocates, including the American Society for Reproductive Medicine, have called for change there, too. It makes absolutely no sense for anti-choice activists to sit by while fertility clinics toss out hundreds of thousands of frozen embryos, but then claim outrage when a handful are used to cure disease.

While no one seems to be keeping close track, it is estimated that there are between 200,000–400,000 frozen embryos in clinics today awaiting their fate. Perhaps more will be used for research in the coming years, but there is another alternative that patients could choose: donation to other infertile couples who can't use their own egg and sperm. While the fertility patients ultimately decide what will happen to their leftovers, less than 3 percent of unused embryos are actually donated. I guess it comes down to whether the thought of a stranger raising your genetic child is creepier than the thought of a clinician pouring your unused embryos down a metal sink drain. Apparently, most people choose the sink.

The overpowering desire to replicate oneself overshadows the personal ethics of pursuing ART for many want-to-be parents. New research is indicating that several birth defects of the heart, esophagus, colon, and cleft palate are two to four times more likely in a single baby conceived via ART. (5) More research is needed, but those are not good early numbers. In addition, while ART is successful less than 30 percent of the time, more than one-third of these "successes" result in a multiple birth. (6) The financial burden of such a birth coupled with the increased likelihood of defects and dangers to the mother are risks we rarely hear about. For example, the number-one cause for premature delivery in the U.S. is multiple births. Over half of all twins and 90 percent of all triplets are born prematurely, and thanks to fertility treatments such births are up 70 percent since 1980. (7) While modern medicine is getting better at saving preemies, a fact sheet released by the American Society for Reproductive Medicine pointed out that there might be a long-term cost. Poor lung development, poor blood circulation in the brain, malnutrition in the womb, cerebral palsy, and increased mortality in the first year of life are all dangers for multiples. (8) A new study published in 2008 in the *Journal of the American Medical Association* has scientists adding early childhood death and adult infertility to the already known long-term dangers. (9) The irony here is that these types of developmental problems are often cited by potential parents as reasons for shying away from adoption! Somewhere there is a break in the information chain, and my suspicion is that the multi-billion-dollar fertility business just may be the culprit, coupled with selfish, desperate potential parents who hear only what they want to hear, and thus put themselves and their offspring at risk simply to ensure that the baby has their eyes, nose, or whatever.

But all of this ugliness is hidden away, and multiple births are portrayed on television and in other media as blessed events. In 1997, Bobbi and Kenny McCaughey welcomed the first living set of septuplets. During the high-risk pregnancy, the couple was counseled about multi-fetal pregnancy reduction (MFPR), a procedure used to reduce the number of growing embryos in a multiple pregnancy. They refused the procedure saying they would leave it in God's hands. Never mind that they took their ability to conceive in the first place out of God's hands when Bobbi took fertility drugs, and now they have seven children, two with cerebral palsy, and others have struggled with developmental and learning problems. Yet when the septuplets were born, they were celebrated. The family received a 5,500-square-foot house, diapers for the first two years, free nanny services, and a congratulatory phone call from then-President Bill Clinton.

The reality show "Jon & Kate Plus 8" celebrated yet another selfishly motivated multiple birth. Jon and Kate Gosselin already had one set of healthy twins born with the help of fertility drugs, but that apparently wasn't enough. In order to have a third child, Kate took more fertility drugs and ended up with sextuplets. How this may affect the first two kids or the long-term problems the sextuplets may have remains to be seen. However, taking such a risk with her life and the lives of her children was even less necessary for her than for the infertile couples out there with zero kids. Regardless, they were rewarded with their own reality TV show that enjoyed Super Bowl-sized ratings!

Unfortunately, turning this family into a media spectacle has been yet another bad decision the Gosselins made. In early 2009, Jon and Kate's marriage started to fall apart, and with cameras rolling they filed for divorce. Yet, even as the public began to turn on the parents for exploiting their kids, the decision to have eight kids in the first place has not been questioned.

While the public watched the Gosselins implode, yet another couple with sextuplets has been given a reality show. Bryan and Jenny Masche agreed to participate in a series about their six children, even though Jon and Kate were already in deep trouble. In an interview with the *New York Daily News*, Jenny said, "I think we're both wise enough to learn from those mistakes [of the Gosselins], instead of thinking, 'Well, that would never happen to us.'" For the sake of their six kids, hopefully these won't be "famous last words."

Not all parents of multiples get the Bobbi and Kenny, Jon and Kate, or Bryan and Jenny treatment, however. After having six consecutive children by IVF, three of whom are disabled, Nadya Suleman went for number seven and ended up with eight. Not eight total, of course, eight at once. The octuplets were the result of an IVF treatment where six embryos were implanted and two apparently divided. Unemployed and living with her parents, Nadya already had far more than she could handle. When asked why she had so many children, given her lack of a partner and inability to care for them financially, Nadya said she had always wanted to have a big family so she could feel connected to another person in a way that was lacking in her own upbringing. It was the desire to fix her own unhappy childhood that led to the incubation of eight premature infants in intensive care, with an estimated cost to California taxpayers of well over a million dollars. Whether or not Nadya will be able to keep all of those children once they have been home for a while is an open question, but surely they will require additional state assistance, as do the three disabled children she already has. The drama surrounding this woman and her financial woes, family discord, and accusations of an obsession with plastic surgery overshadowed what could have been a much needed public debate on the ethics of ARTs.

In an interview with Ann Curry on NBC News, Nadya Suleman said that it was her lifestyle and status as a single mom that drew such a backlash against her, and she may be right. Had Nadya's eight babies been born to a nice, well-to-do married couple like the McCaugheys or the Masches, the story probably would have been very different. The dangers of the procedure and the selfish risk-taking undergone by the mother would not have even entered the debate. Yet rather than a defense, this fact should make us rethink our cultural glorification of multiple births, specifically those created via ARTs.

When a woman undergoes any form of ART and winds up with a litter (three or more) in her womb, the very survival of some may demand the elimination of others. In such cases, a procedure called multi-fetal pregnancy reduction (MFPR) is often recommended. In MFPR, a physician injects the selected fetus or fetuses with potassium chloride to stop the heartbeat. Because it is done very early in the pregnancy, the fetus is usually absorbed by the mother's body. The ethical and emotional implications of such a procedure are surely heart-wrenching for couples who often have struggled for years just to get pregnant at all.

However, the glorified parents of multiple births we have been seeing all over television share one common claim. They all insist that MFPR was not an option. Due to their faith in God, none would consider this procedure. But where was their trust in God when they couldn't get pregnant to begin with? Obviously, they didn't mind playing God in order to get pregnant, yet when faced with the consequences of that, they deferred to the Divine Creator. The decision to pass on MFPR is certainly understandable, but citing the will of God as the reason screams of hypocrisy. Unfortunately, the babies pay the physical price with long-term disabilities, provided they make it through infanthood. Currently, the Centers for Disease Control and Prevention do not collect data on MFPR, so the frequency of its use is unknown.

As the billion-dollar baby-making machine grinds on, the U.S. Department of Health and Human Services reports that of the half a million children in foster care, well over one hundred thirty thousand are waiting permanent adoption (10), while about forty thousand babies are born each year via IVF. If these parents chose adoption instead, there would be plenty of orphans to go around. No wonder many childfrees see the attitude of those who pursue a genetically linked baby by any means necessary as being selfish.

But you don't have to be infertile to experience the medical big business of making babies. In her documentary, *The Business of Being Born*, two-time mom Ricki Lake explores our nation's current birthing model and whom it is benefiting. Although we have one of the highest rates of both maternal and infant mortality in the industrialized world, the myth that America's healthcare system is second to none prevails. Hospital births began in the early 1900s as an alternative to home births, and since that time the medicalization of the birth process has succeeded in convincing women that they are incapable of doing what nature has prepared them to do for millions of years—give birth. In Europe and Japan, when the delivery of babies was moved into hospitals, midwives followed. Today, 70 percent of the births in those countries are performed by qualified midwives, with the doctor only around to deal with true complications. Compare this to 8 percent in the U.S. and it begs the question: if doctors are so good at deliveries, why don't we have a lower mortality rate? (11) The answer is simple, according to Lake who makes a strong argument that the protocol for delivering babies in the U.S. benefits doctors, hospitals, and insurance companies at the expense of mothers and babies. Here are some of the facts she clues women into and your pregnant friends should know:

- Hospitals often market themselves as being open to various birthing plans, but rarely deviate from their one-size-fits-all protocol. (12)
- The number of births by C-section increases at four P.M. and ten P.M., ensuring that the obstetrician is home in time for dinner, or at least not up all night. (13)
- Cesarean sections are also up 46 percent since 1996 and now account for one in three deliveries. Due to fear of litigation, doctors often rush to this option, regardless of the fact that major complications can and do arise. (14)
- When women question interventions being implemented that they didn't want, they are simply told it is for the good of the baby. Who would argue? However, women are disempowered by that statement and make decisions based on fear rather than fact. (15)

- Mothers who are given epidurals have longer labors and are often given the drug Pitocin to speed things up. The Pitocin intensifies the contractions so much that the epidural is then turned up, slowing things down again and thus requiring more Pitocin. This sets up a cycle that frequently results in a distressed baby and an emergency C-section. (16)
- Pitocin blocks the natural brain chemical cocktail known as oxytocin, which has been crafted by nature over millions of years to keep the mother's focus on the protection and nourishment of the child and imprinting the mother/child bond. (17)
- Another reason for interventions such as Pitocin, C-sections, and others is the straight-up business side of the equation. Hospitals don't want women hanging around the delivery room too long; they want them in and out and on to the next one. Bottom-line issues place the care of mother and baby below the importance of profit, a systemic problem in our health-care system that goes far beyond childbearing. (18)
- The cost of a hospital delivery is thirteen thousand dollars, while the cost of a home birth with a qualified midwife is about four thousand dollars. Hospitals continue to scare women out of this option, even though the outcomes of home births are as good as or better than those of hospital births. (19)

The self-interest of the free-market health-care system is the beneficiary of the status quo, not mothers and babies. It cannot be said that children come first when the whole system of bringing them into this world—be it via fertility treatments, hospital deliveries, or both—is shrouded in misinformation, intimidation, and outright lies that actually hurt mothers and babies in the name of profit.

While the facts continue to chip away at the façade of our self-sacrificing, child-centered society, the idealized version of what a family is pressures women to undergo extreme measures to reach the perceived pinnacle of womanhood—being a mother. It also emboldens parents to expect reverence and entitlements, regardless of the fact that they made a choice to be parents based on their own pursuit of happiness, just like the child-free. Being a good parent today is tough, and those who choose this path do deserve respect. Yet once a woman has succumbed to society's demands and created new life, she can be sure that someone out there will still think she's doing it wrong, no matter what child-rearing choices she makes. The criticisms she endures, however, will most likely come from an unexpected source—other moms.

MOM VERSUS MOM

The childfree often feel beleaguered by their parenting peers, fending off criticism and constantly defending themselves. But even women who have become mothers are constantly being drafted into public warfare against each other where they can't win. In the age of "my way or the highway," the so-called mommy wars publicly pit career moms against stay-at-home moms in a thirteen-round fight to the finish. This doesn't exactly sweeten the pot for those women on the childbearing fence.

"With the child-centric nature of things these days, you have parents dogging other parents for not having the right style and it's just a whole culture of things that I don't want to have anything to do with," explained Jennifer H., a twenty-nine-year-old law student.

The Mommy Wars started in the early '90s, when stories about women being pulled between work and home ignited a feud between career moms and stay-at-home moms. But like many public debates disguised as meaningful dialogue, this was nothing but a fabricated controversy that has lasted well into the new millennium. Tapping into women's insecurities and then getting them to turn on each other makes for very entertaining and profitable television, but that's about it. The only ones who seem to benefit from the ongoing mommy wars are parenting magazines and talk shows that periodically remind mothers they are letting themselves and/or their children down.

Louise, a thirty-nine-year-old speech therapist, related, *"My cousin shared with me that in her world there are only two camps—working moms and stay-at-home moms—and they don't get along with each other. It's a huge thing for her. So even if you have children, you end up getting discriminated against based on what choices you make as a mother. We are very unforgiving in our culture."*

In her 2005 book, *The Truth behind the Mommy Wars*, Miriam Peskowitz frames the problem as a labor issue. She complains that mothers want more choices and more freedom around parenting and work in the rigid corporate environment. Actually, so do many childfrees! There was a time in recent history when decisions were easier. Women could be mothers, teachers, librarians, nurses, or secretaries. When they married, they were expected to leave the workplace to raise a family—and that, as they say, was that. Thanks to the women's movement of the '60s and '70s, this is no longer the case, and none of us want to go back to those "easy" choices. But today, while we are so fortunate to have almost countless life paths available to us, some limits still remain. Saying yes to one path often means saying no to another.

Parents should take responsibility for raising their children, but before having them they should know that it's a job that requires some sacrifices. Yet, supporting a work environment that is more flexible is not just in the interests of parents. Interesting and well-paid part-time work is hard to come by, and as we saw in the previous chapter, the forty-hour week that was once considered full time is quickly being replaced by sixty- to eighty-hour workweeks. Working less than whatever is now considered full time also carries the problem of benefit loss, including health insurance, unemployment insurance, and Social Security.

The fact is that most part-time work in this country is low-wage work with no benefits. But parents and non-parents alike may have a lot to contribute to society if given the option of well-paid, benefited part-time work. Parents would have better work/life balance, thus raising healthier children. Non-parents would be able to support themselves while building up a new business or other creative endeavor. Most job creation in this country, after all, comes from small businesses. Both groups would also be able to pursue other creative endeavors such as art, music, writing, or whatever dreams they may have. These things, in the end, make our society more humane and our country a better place to live for all generations.

When parents grow tired of what feels like limited options around work, they should know that lots of childfrees feel the same way. It is not a dilemma for just parents to figure out, but for all of us. There is no final answer as to whether working moms or stay-at-home moms are making the best choice. That is because the real war is not mom versus mom, but the individual versus a very narrow and inflexible workplace. However, the status quo benefits the corporate machines, and without a grassroots cultural revolution that is unlikely to change any time soon.

In 2006, Leslie Morgan Steiner tried to settle the debate once and for all when she published *Mommy Wars,* wherein twenty-six happy stay-at-home and working moms told their stories in an attempt to better understand and respect each other. By 2007, it seemed that perhaps the mommy wars had run their course. But just when moms thought they might be able to put down the bayonets, along came Alaska Governor Sarah Palin to ignite the debate all over again.

Once she was nominated for the 2008 Republican vice presidential ticket, stories about Governor Palin's five children—one with special needs and another seventeen and pregnant—began to surface and raise questions as to how a mom could manage all that plus the demanding VP job. Interestingly, many of the criticisms of Palin came from other mothers, and the temporary cease-fire ended. Accusations of parental neglect were countered with accusations of sexism. How could Palin be a good mom and still be a heartbeat away from the presidency? Why were we asking these questions of Palin and not of the male candidates? If she spent more time at home, would she have a pregnant seventeen-year-old daughter? What about her infant with Down syndrome? Opinions for and against Palin as a working mom came from both sides of the political spectrum and persisted through the election. Had she won, I am sure these questions would have continued to been raised, but with the defeat of McCain-Palin the debate seems to be quieting. For now the mommy wars controversy lies dormant, at least until the next opportunity for the media to promote its self-interest by inciting the fight once again.

The financial rewards of pitting women against each other have lined the media moguls' pockets for ages, causing well-documented damage to women's psychological well-being. Whether it's mom versus mom, a Miss Whoever beauty pageant, or a bunch of gals competing for some has-been rock star on a reality show, women have been told the score. If you want to succeed you must outfox your sisters and land the title, the man, or whatever. The endless, unattainable images of beauty and perfection hurled at women are contrived to make us feel lacking, undesirable, and less worthy than our peers. The benefits of the girl-on-girl media catfights are reaped by the media itself, the television networks, and the endless suppliers of diet/fashion/beauty products designed to make us better than the rest. Making women feel bad about themselves so that they will buy things is a hazard that has resulted in an epidemic of low self-esteem. While measuring self-esteem is challenging due to the nuanced definitions out there, it is estimated that at least two-thirds of women suffer from low self-esteem. Research has shown that this leads to all sorts of self-destructive behavior, including promiscuity, drug abuse, and eating disorders in a society constantly trying to sell women an unattainable ideal. This hazard has also fully infiltrated the realm of motherhood, creating an environment of "competitive parenting" that is very profitable for the child-rearing industry.

SUPERMOM

While the "battle" between stay-at-home moms and career moms plays out in the collective imagination, another ridiculous, make-believe menace hangs over both groups' heads. In a blur of energy, the idealized "supermom" makes the images of pink-cheeked children in spotless clothing sitting quietly in an impeccably kept house actually attainable. While the media was busy boosting circulation and ratings by starting the preemptive mommy wars, the advertisers found a way to strike fear into the hearts of the women whose insecurity they breed, putting many dollars in their pockets. It is not enough to make women feel self-conscious about their bodies with fashion magazines sporting double-zero waifs; advertisers must also make sure every mother feels incompetent and inadequate should she not buy the latest hot baby product. This leads to a lot of peer pressure among supermoms who want to believe that some baby product will actually make their impossible life seem possible, their ordinary child seem extraordinary.

For instance, every parent knows that if you don't get your newborn on Baby Einstein immediately, you will certainly seal their fate as a flunkey. The vague, unsupported claims of value the makers of this supposedly educational tool, now owned by Disney, purport on their Web site are astounding. First, they flout the recommendations of the American Academy of Pediatrics, which recommends that babies not watch anything on a screen before the age of two. (After all, what does the American Academy of Pediatrics know about children?) Next, they inform parents—in language so soothing that it is easy to miss its insidious nature—that they respectfully disagree and truly don't believe television is harmful before the age of two. Not one study to back up their claim is referenced or cited. Of course, they fully respect a parent's right to make his or her own decisions about whether or not to use television. (Wow! You still have the right to make your own decisions about TV? What a company!) It's reminiscent of tobacco executives sitting before Congress and claiming that cigarettes aren't bad for you, based on nothing but their own opinions (not to mention financial interests). Parents are being pressured into buying products with the promise of developmental benefits that not only don't deliver what's promised, but are potentially harmful—and it ain't just the paint!

In August 2007, *Time* magazine reported a study done at the University of Washington which found that for each hour spent tripping on the morphing images those Baby Einstein DVDs produce, babies understood an average of seven fewer words than their non-tripping counterparts. (20) Bad news for parents who spent over two hundred million dollars on the Baby Einstein series last year. (21)

While supermom images present a model that is as unattainable as that double-zero jeans size, it won't stop women from trying to pursue them both. The supermoms' fear is that they will scar their children for life if they don't buy into the latest gimmick, if they set boundaries, or if they dare to say no. The effects on society are already being seen, as the early offspring of the supermom is just coming of age and entering the workforce. These self-proclaimed wonder kids have created a real challenge to their baby boomer and gen-X employers by expecting constant praise and flattery and rejecting any limits or boundaries. Apparently, being raised in an environment that lavishes gold stars on you just for showing up, ends every T-ball game in a tie, and never tells you no, doesn't prepare you to deal with the complexities of the entry-level work world. Quite a shock for both employee and employer.

According to the "60 Minutes" story, "The Millennials Are Coming" (November 11, 2007), companies around the country are hiring consultants and rethinking their culture in order to handle the new wave of kudos-seeking young people in the workplace. Born roughly between 1978 and 1995 and now called the Millennium Generation, this new breed of young person is sweeping the job market, throwing the old-school "all work and no play" work ethic on its ear. Unlike previous generations who lived to work, the Millennials work to live. Maybe that's not such a bad thing, given our work habits discussed in the previous chapter. Yet while on the surface supermoms seem willing to do anything for their kids, they also are willing to send supposedly grown men and women out into the world who have never taken care of their personal needs, never been told no, and/or never been denied undivided attention.

The competitive parenting bred by the supermom does have a dark side. It is not just about being all that you can be for your children and family, it is about being better than everybody else. Having the superstar child becomes an obsession, and the supermom submits to a life of competitive parenting for her prodigy in the making.

Vicki, a buyer in the automotive industry, feels sorry for these kids. *"There's a lot of pressure on kids that stems from parents being so competitive. They are put in way too many extracurricular activities. In addition to homework, they have soccer, gymnastics, hockey, etc. I think the parents do it more for themselves than they do for the kids. I see sad, stressed-out-looking kids and I don't think it's fair to them."*

Rather than enjoying their healthy, normal kids, supermoms buy into whatever scam is being hocked, just so the Joneses' kid doesn't get ahead of theirs. Most parents want to do what is best for their kids, but what is "best" changes and morphs along with research, trends, and marketing needs. This confuses even the most well-meaning parents and often leaves them feeling guilty for not doing it "right."

Breastfeeding, for example, is something that was good, then bad, then good again, and now feels compulsory to most new moms. In a 2009 article for *The Atlantic,* Hanna Rosin shares her experience with other mothers on the playground when she told them she might stop breast-feeding after a month or two. "The air of insta-friendship we had established cooled into an icy politeness, and the mothers shortly wandered away...." (22) Was this merely a fluke? To find out, she tried the same thing on other groups of mothers and sadly experienced similar reactions. On a quest to find out if this social scorning was really warranted, Rosin did an extensive review of the medical research and found that the medical journals and popular media were telling two different stories when it came to the benefits of breastfeeding. While popular media would credit breastfeeding for the prevention of every ailment under the sun, the medical research found loose connections at best. With no definitive conclusions found by science, then, it becomes the job of popular culture to dictate what moms should do—and God help any woman who makes the "wrong" choice.

In the article, Rosin goes on to ask if there are any downsides to breastfeeding, and observes that while we threw off the shackles of the Hoover vacuum cleaner so necessary for 1950s housewifery, women are now shackled by another sucking sound. "When people say that breastfeeding is 'free,' I want to hit them with a two-by-four. It's only free if a woman's time is worth nothing." And just like that, we are back to the mommy wars, in which women who choose to give up a year of corporate climbing to breastfeed are betraying the women's movement and women who don't are damaging their kids with formula. Invalidating someone else's choice to justify one's own is nothing new, but when mothers do it to each other they don't just hurt their fellow moms, but the kids, too. A parent who feels bad about herself, or suffers low self-esteem, can't very well instill high self-esteem and confidence into a child.

Unfortunately, the supermom phenomenon does not end with educational toys, poor boundaries, or breastfeeding debates. Once those kids go on solid food there's a whole other army waiting to tear parents apart. The "food fascist supermom" would have anyone daring to poison her child with non-organic food tarred and feathered. While we all may need to pay closer attention to what is going into our food, the organic supermom has taken it to the extreme.

In an article for The Daily Beast Web site, Laura Bennett relates her horror at just such a mom who was attempting to have her ex-husband's joint custody revoked for the unforgivable sin of packing their kids a non-organic lunch. This "food Nazi" mom, as Bennett called her, was actually going to attempt to deny her kids access to their father over a bag of Cheetos, a Go-GURT, and a sandwich made on white bread. In contrast, Bennett argued, it is far more important to teach kids decision-making skills than to deprive them of all things "bad." According to Bennett, these sheltered kids are often out of control when in an environment where junk food is available. (23)

When I read about the scrutiny, judgment, and criticism that befall mothers, I realize that the ridiculous objections hurled at the childfree are part of a bigger cultural problem that seems to get its jollies by criticizing women. Have children, don't have children; either way, you will be judged for something. The selfish one is not the parent or non-parent, but the person who engages in this kind of dissonance to justify his or her own choices.

But whatever parenting trends we are experiencing today, they are unlikely to deter the masses from parenthood any time soon. After all, the drive to procreate is one of the strongest and most powerful of human drives, at least for some of us. Up until recently, the assumption of reproduction was unquestioned. However, for a growing number of women and men, the appeal of having children—sometimes by horrific means—then spending lots of time, money, and energy trying to do it "right," only to end up falling short of someone's expectations, is lacking. Instead, they are turning their nurturing energy toward society at large, contributing in other ways to the greater good.

RANDOM ACTS OF KINDNESS

In his book *The Empty Cradle*, Phillip Longman wonders what Microsoft would be today if Bill Gates's mother had chosen not to have children. This is the type of comment that drives me crazy, because one could just as easily wonder what the world would be like if Adolph Hitler's mother had decided she didn't want children. Tit for tat. Rather than living in "what ifs," I prefer to look at what is, and the truth is that childfree people make amazing contributions to society. Whether it is the respite care we provide friends and relatives from their parental obligations, volunteering in local communities, picking up the slack for child-burdened coworkers, committing to social causes, or working toward healthier, more sustainable communities, the labors of the non-parent contribute to making this country great. Some of these contributions, believe it or not, actually directly benefit parents and children.

Holly, a forty-five-year-old garden shop owner, is known as "Auntie Holly" to the neighborhood kids, and provides much-appreciated support to the parents on her street. Eileen is more than a forty-eight-year-old journeyman printer; she is an activist for justice who is most proud of her success in negotiating better maternity leave benefits for women in her profession. Viki is only twenty-nine, but between working in an architectural firm, performing as a classically trained singer, and working on her graduate degree, she still finds time to volunteer as the assistant director of the children's folk dancing and singing group in her local German club. Then there's Shannon, a thirty-five-year-old paralegal who has volunteered doing singles outreach in her church, working with physically and mentally challenged teens, and heading up her local area March of Dimes walkathon.

But it seems no matter what the childfree achieve or how great a contribution they make to society, there are still some out there who see childfrees as falling short by not creating human capital. This is especially true of those ensconced in traditional organized religion. Viki found that one out for herself. *"I've been spending some time with the wives of my husband's friends who probably think that I'm going to hell. One day they were talking about wanting to have children and how selfish it would be not to, so I brought up the environment and how there were too many people on the planet already. One of them turned to me and said, 'I'd rather have a van full of Christian children than a tree in my yard.' Too bad her kids won't have any trees to climb in."*

Although Jesus was childfree (according to the official version, anyway) the altruistic, compassionate actions of many childfrees fall short of some Christians' expectations of women. In Marlene's case, this came as a rude awakening. Now fifty-three years old and happily married for twenty of those years, she has worked her entire life to better the lives of others and has a long and distinguished career with many nonprofit organizations. *"We were living in California, where I had been doing fundraising work for a local hospital. There was a board member I worked closely with, and I had many occasions to go to his home for meetings and whatnot. He and his wife were getting on in years, and they had in their employ a retired nun working as a caregiver to the family. We developed a friendly relationship, and I grew to like her very much. She knew I was married, and so one day she asked me how many children I had. I told her I didn't have any children, and she seemed taken aback. 'But you're married, right?' 'Yes, I am married,' I told her, 'but we aren't going to have children.' Astonished, she began to fire away at me, asking why I was married if I didn't want children. After all, the only reason to be married was to procreate. She said there was a little baby up in heaven just waiting to be born to me, and I was selfishly keeping that soul out of this world! Well, my jaw just dropped and I had no idea what to say. I had never been called on the carpet that way. I resorted to lying and told her that my husband couldn't give me children. 'Oh, well, that's different,' she recanted. I was just so appalled by the interrogation and then by my need to lie about it. At that young age, I just didn't have an answer to that."*

Regardless of what some in the traditional religious community think, many women without children are raising the level of consciousness on our planet by using their energies to create a better world for us all. As one of the most recognizable childfree women today, Oprah Winfrey is an irrefutable example of how childfrees can serve humanity in a broad and meaningful way. The list of people she has helped would fill volumes. The Oprah Winfrey Leadership Academy for Girls, which opened in January 2007, welcomed three hundred girls into an environment where they can thrive and grow. At the ceremony welcoming the school's first class, she said, *"For many years, people have always asked me why didn't I have children. Now I know why I didn't have children, because I have all of these daughters."* (24) In addition to her growing number of students, Oprah quietly and remotely parents ten African children whom she supports with housing, caregivers, private schools, etc. In a *USA Weekend* magazine article, she was asked why she didn't bring the kids over here like some other high-profile celebrities have done. Her reply was, *"If I didn't have a day job, I absolutely would have made a different decision. I didn't bring these kids over here* [because] *my lifestyle is not such that I could devote all my time to these children, and that is what would need to happen."* (25) By remaining physically childfree, she ensures that many more people will benefit from her presence on this earth. She not only does the work of giving, she sets an example for all of us blessed with good fortune of how easy it is to change the lives of others. In a troubled world, what more could we ask from anyone?

The contributions of the childfree cannot be denied. By being available to a friend or family member for babysitting, volunteering in the community, taking part in philanthropy, running the businesses that keep our economy going, or just being conscious enough to know that bringing an unwanted child into the world would be a tragedy for at least two lives, we childfree are as motivated as parents to create a better tomorrow—even with no heir to pass it on to. One can hardly call that selfish.

Most of us really want the same thing—a healthy, happy, peaceful world. While we may have different ideas about how to get there, it is important to understand that we all play a part. Parents provide the human capital that makes up the next generation, and it takes a lot of effort, time, and money to do so. The childfree are also an integral part of our society and work hard to make it a better world for the next generation. When we refuse to create a divide and respect each other's unique role, everyone comes out a winner.

Some of us are meant to have children and some are not, plain and simple. The notion that we all must procreate is outdated and unnecessary. It is one side of two extreme opposites, because the antithesis of the belief that *everyone* should have children is the belief that *no one* should. The Voluntary Human Extinction Movement (VHEMT) has taken this extremist position, as laid out on their Web site, www.vhemt.org:

The hopeful alternative to the extinction of millions of species of plants and animals is the voluntary extinction of one species: Homo sapiens...us. Each time another one of us decides to not add another one of us to the burgeoning billions already squatting on this ravaged planet, another ray of hope shines through the gloom. When every human chooses to stop breeding, Earth's biosphere will be allowed to return to its former glory, and all remaining creatures will be free to live, die, evolve (if they believe in evolution), and will perhaps pass away, as so many of Nature's "experiments" have done throughout the eons.

With many of us now "volunteering" and opting out of parenthood, the more likely result will be a reduction in population to a more manageable level. There are quite enough of us now to sustain the human race, and too many more of us could be devastating to our planet. Devout Christians and other religious people see the prevention of children as a sin against God, but they never consider that perhaps it was Divine intervention that inspired the development of birth control right about the time our planet had all the humans it could handle.

Childfree people are often very mindful of their ecological footprint and see the mass consumption of resources by parents and their offspring as more evidence of their selfishness. For example, according to The Green Guide, parents change up to 8,000 disposable diapers per child, resulting in 3.5 million tons of landfill waste each year. In addition, the creation of the one-time-use nappies consumes 250,000 trees per year and the bleaching process used on the wood pulp creates elevated levels of dioxin, a toxic chemical. It is illegal to dispose of human waste in a landfill because of possible groundwater contamination and other potential health hazards, but when it comes to disposable diapers, this law is not enforced.

Almost everyone I interviewed for this book cited the problem of overpopulation as either one reason for or at least a benefit of their decision. With all of the concerns about pollution, global warming, diminishing resources, and so on, I wonder if the planet can tolerate many more of us. We will look at the issues surrounding population, birth control, and the role of religion in the next chapter.

3
It's Your Duty to Go Forth and Multiply!

The most effective form of birth control I know is spending the day with my kids.

—Jill Bensley

The children are the future, as they say, and having children has historically been seen as a responsibility, not a choice. For many women and men, even in modern society, the assumption of reproduction persists, whether the pressure is from peers or parents. This ignores the reality that with over 6.8 billion Homo sapiens roaming the globe, the obsession with procreation may be leading us toward our own destruction. While discussions of overpopulation and its potential hazards go back a couple of centuries, it was the publication of *The Population Bomb* in 1968 by Paul R. Ehrlich that brought attention to the subject. The book hypothesized that overpopulation would lead to the starvation of hundreds of millions of people in the 1970s and 1980s, a prediction that did not come to pass. Some anti-environmentalists have used this fact as proof that our current environmental concerns are inherently flawed and that our ever-expanding presence on this planet can continue unabated. However, the projections Ehrlich made were a warning of what *might* happen should the growth rate of the day remain constant. It did not. The global birthrate of 4.6 children per woman in 1968 has sharply declined to 2.6 today. (1) That and the advances in agriculture are likely reasons the great famines never materialized. Perhaps, whether we meant to or not, we averted some of the disasters Ehrlich predicted, which is the point of an advance warning, right?

When *The Population Bomb* was published in 1968, there were 3.5 billion people on the planet. Today, even with the sharp decline in global birthrates, we are up to 6.8 billion, and whether or not the disasters predicted by Ehrlich ever come true, your average high school student could tell you that at some point we will reach maximum capacity, if we haven't already.

The Old Testament directive about going forth and multiplying that God allegedly handed down to Adam and Eve may have made a lot of sense when there was a sum total of *two* people on the entire planet!

And God blessed them, and God said unto them, be fruitful and multiply, and replenish the earth, and subdue it: and have dominion over the fish of the sea, and over the fowl of the air, and over every living thing that moveth upon the earth. Genesis 1:28

But what about today, with our six and a half billion human inhabitants, and rising? Every time you sit in traffic on the freeway or wait in line at your local grocer, you probably feel like we have replenished our earth within an inch of its life! And we have. For a current, up-to-the-second estimate of the global population, you can visit www.census.gov/ipc/www/popclockworld.html and watch the world population clock tick up 2.4 people per second, 147 per minute, 8,814 per hour, 211,546 per day, and a mind-boggling 77,214,435 per year. I think we've got the "fruitful and multiply" thing covered. As for dominion over the fish of the sea, fowl in the air, and every living thing that moveth upon the earth—well, we really ran with that one. In a 2006 article for *Time* magazine, science reporter Unmesh Kher reported that the all-you-can-eat seafood buffet will soon be closing unless we temper our tastes for the ocean's bounty. (2) Citing a report released from Dalhousie University, Kher reported that the seafood supply will be depleted by mid-century. (3) Researchers at the university, led by marine biologist Boris Worm, studied many variables, including global catch rates, and calculated that by 2050 seafood will be far too expensive and rare for the average consumer.

The creatures of the deep aren't the only ones endangered by humans' voracious appetites, either. A study published in 2004 in the science journal *Nature* reported that the combination of rising global temperatures along with the existing habitat threats many species face have put more than a million species at risk for extinction by 2050. (4) Species of both land and sea are not the only resources in jeopardy of being strained or depleted. Human "progress" has also put a strain on energy supplies, drinking water, forests, minerals, and other natural treasures.

"I don't really understand the push to put more and more people on this planet. Over the years, the population has been

growing exponentially, creating pollution, greenhouse gases, global warming, and a strain on resources," reasons twenty-nine-year-old Jennifer H.

IS IT HOT IN HERE?

The increasing human presence on planet Earth has led to some alarming realities. In his book *The Future of Life*, Pulitzer Prize–winning author and scientist Edward O. Wilson reveals that, while the ecological footprint for the entire human race averages about 5.2 acres per person, the American average is about 24 acres per person. He does the math, which reveals that under current technologies the job of raising all of humanity to the American standard of living would require four more planet Earths! (5) Meanwhile, the rapid industrialization and Americanization of developing nations around the globe, most notably in places such as India and China, barrels on as if the laws of physics simply don't apply. Concerns over the rapid industrialization around the world and the strain it puts on resources are second to the more immediate danger it creates. With more industry comes more carbon dioxide (CO_2), and with more CO_2 comes more global warming.

In America, global warming is quickly moving out of the realm of the controversial and into the realm of accepted science. Our realization of this fact is only about a decade behind those of most other industrialized nations. Sure, you still have your Pat Buchanans and other delusional holdouts, who continue to insist it is all a big hoax. And yes, irresponsible claims like his have contributed to our much-delayed response to this crisis. However, such voices are sounding ever more foolish in the face of the overwhelming scientific consensus. Global warming is not just the result of too many people; there are too many pollutants, with the big enemy being CO_2.

We now know that the increased CO_2 emissions from burning fossil fuels have created a greenhouse effect, thickening our atmosphere and trapping warmer air inside it. As the climate warms, plants, animals, and water respond by moving toward the still cooler poles. Droughts, heat waves, and fires occur more frequently, storms become more powerful, and—perhaps most alarming—glaciers begin to drip, drip, drip into the sea. Rising sea levels have already led to the evacuation of many inhabitants from low-lying Pacific Island nations and made beachfront property owners out of townsfolk in northeast England. Another study estimated that the beaches of Spain will shrink an estimated fifty feet by the year 2050, as the sands are washed under rising seas by ever more powerful waves. (6) While the melting of free-floating glaciers presents a problem for low-lying islands and coasts, a larger danger for all of us is the loss of land-based ice shelves. Much like dropping ice cubes into a full glass of water, land-based ice shelves falling into the sea could cause a more rapid worldwide event as the seas spill over coastlines on a global scale.

The increased presence of meltwater atop land-based ice shelves in places like Greenland and Antarctica is an enormous cause for concern. Environmental champion and Nobel Prize winner Al Gore explains in his book, later made into an Oscar–winning documentary, *An Inconvenient Truth*: "In Greenland, as in the Antarctic Peninsula, this meltwater is now believed to keep sinking all the way down to the bottom, cutting deep crevasses and vertical tunnels that scientists call 'moulins.' When the water reaches the bottom of the ice, it lubricates the surface of the bedrock and destabilizes the ice mass, raising fears that the ice mass will slide more quickly toward the ocean." This takes the analogy of dropping ice cubes into a full glass of water to a whole new level. Just as the displaced water pours over the rim of the glass, the slippage of a large-enough ice shelf into the sea would cause oceans to drown our coasts in nearly an instant. While this may seem quite alarmist, it is important to note that a thirty-by-one-hundred-dred-fifty-mile section of the ice shelf on the Antarctic Peninsula, known as Larsen-B, broke apart and fell into the sea in a matter of days, despite the belief that that it would be stable for at least a century. (7) This event led to the discovery of moulins and the resulting bedrock lubrication concerns. Should even larger pieces of the ice shelves slip into the sea, the damage along every inch of coast worldwide would be worse than that inflicted by Hurricane Katrina. No wonder some holdouts cling to the hoax theory. The reality option is not just inconvenient, it's incomprehensible.

To reduce the CO_2 emissions, cool the planet, and avert disaster, what we need are fewer pollutants, which also means fewer people. Currently, most industrialized nations are actually seeing a decline in population, with fertility rates falling below the replacement rate of 2.1 children per woman. For example, Italy and Germany both currently have a fertility rate of 1.3; Canada's is 1.6; and Japan's is 1.2. The U.S. is holding steady at 2.0, largely due to immigration from countries where large families are the norm. With an ecological footprint of twenty-four acres, the largest on the planet, and a current population of more than 350 million people, not bringing another consuming American into the world is a good start on conservation. After all, a child born in the U.S. will consume about five times the global average in resources. However, as the industrialization of other parts of the world continues, the ecological footprint for all of humanity rises.

Janet, a marketing manager for a large tech company, is glad she's not adding to the wastefulness inherent in raising a child in America. "*My sister is fairly affluent, and they will have a kid party where they invite about twenty-five six-year-olds over. Each one brings a present, and then each guest receives a goody bag that is full of all sorts of cheap plastic crap from China that my sister buys for pennies. Then the kids take it, look through it, go home and promptly throw it away. I just find that so disgusting. It is just wasteful, crappy consumer-itis. The weird thing is that even my sister feels that way. We were talking about it and she said, 'You don't understand; that is just what everyone does.' So there is this social pressure that you have to keep up with because you don't want your kid to be singled out as not doing what the other kids are doing, but it just fuels consumerism and materialism. Ugh. We* [the childfree] *leave a very light footprint on this earth, largely because we don't have to keep up with what the Joneses are doing with their kids.*"

Western demand for cheap goods made in China has fueled its economy and increased urbanization and industrialization. Concerned environmentalists used to tell us that the U.S. was the number-one emitter of CO_2 in the world, but in 2006 China clinched the title and now leads the charge. (8) It is their rapidly growing economy, and not their relatively low birthrate of 1.7, that is to blame. Former president George W. Bush cited the weaker environmental standards of such emerging nations as his administration's main reason for bowing out of the Kyoto Protocol in 2001, an international climate stabilization treaty ratified by 174 nations and counting. However, the attitude of "we'll stop polluting when they stop polluting" does nothing more than ensure that everyone keeps polluting at the status quo.

One can easily point an accusatory finger at China for its 47 percent increase in emissions or blame rapidly growing India with its 55 percent increase in emissions over the last decade, thus absolving the West of any guilt or responsibility. However, this type of finger-pointing ignores what really has happened. A 2007 study published in the *Proceedings of the National Academy of Sciences (PNAS)* reported that while rapidly industrializing nations such as China and India were responsible for 73 percent of the growth in emissions, it is "largely due to the shift of energy intensive activities from developed to developing nations." (9) Over the past decade it is not just the majority of manufacturing jobs that were outsourced, but the emissions that go along with them. As a result, while the U.S. may no longer be on top of the emissions pile, its ravenous consumer economy fuels the growing pollution abroad in nations with even weaker environmental regulation. In a global economy where production and consumption are irrevocably intertwined, it will matter little who was at fault and matter most who is leading the way to solutions. Even with a more environmentally friendly Obama administration at the helm, we may or may not be able to divert the effects of global warming, so keep a pair of water wings ready!

A WORLD WITH FEWER OF US

Many fear that we are killing our planet, but it is far more likely that it'll kill us long before we can kill it. Suppose for a minute that the planet did just that, and unleashed a virus that killed all humans while sparing all other forms of life. What would happen? Alan Weisman took a look at such a scenario in his book *The World Without Us*, which advocates for a more stable population while showing how the healing power of our planet can overcome many of the destructive attacks Homo sapiens throw at her. Weisman writes about Chernobyl, the site of the 1986 nuclear reactor explosion that killed thousands, made countless others gravely ill, and obliterated forests, plants, and wildlife. Surprisingly, life is returning: birds perch on the radioactive metal arms of abandoned cranes and forests reclaim the scorched land. Even the land animals are returning, with wolves, deer, lynx, and wild boars roaming the thirty-kilometer radius surrounding the reactor known as the Zone of Alienation.

Another alienated zone, the Korean Demilitarized Zone (DMZ), hasn't seen more than the occasional footprint of a desperate, fleeing North Korean for more than fifty years. The result is a virtual mecca of flourishing wildlife that has become the pride and joy of Korean bird watchers and provides a much-needed lifeline for several species on the brink of extinction, such as the Asiatic black bear and the Amur leopard. The beautiful splendor of the two kilometers north and south of the 38th parallel is protected from humans by our own tools of destruction—land mines and razor-wire fencing.

But rather than wipe out the human race, Weisman arrives at a more digestible proposal. If we limited global reproduction to one child per couple, he concludes, the human population would stabilize at 1.6 billion by the end of this century. Perhaps if such an agreement were reached, those of us who are uninterested in reproducing anyway could donate (sell?) our one-child allotment to someone else, thus preserving the sibling relationships many of us hold dear and preventing the creation of an only-child adult population unable to share its toys.

The problem with such a proposal is similar to the problems of eugenics described in chapter 2. In a free society, how can reproduction be regulated? How would a one-child-per-couple policy be enforced? When such a policy was implemented in China, things like forced abortion and forced sterilization were used to ensure compliance. Serious ethical issues would trump any environmental benefit if it were made compulsory; it could only succeed if it were voluntary. It is unlikely that a global agreement on a one-child policy will be happening any time soon.

When asked about our duty to "go forth and multiply," most childfrees will tell you that they see it as an outdated notion. In our not-so-distant past, when infant mortality rates were high and life expectancy was low, breeding large families was crucial for survival. However, when we consider current global population growth and the strain it puts on our planet's health and resources, it is arguable that only by decreasing population can the human race survive. As it turns out, the tide may very well be turning in that direction, however unintentional.

After staring at the population clock for a few minutes, it may be difficult to believe that the sound of global population growth coming to a screeching halt can already be heard. Sure, the world's population is growing in total number, but decreases in fertility rates in both the developed and developing worlds may actually be leading us down the road of a much-needed population decline. Today, global fertility is about 2.6 children per woman, which is less than half of the six children per woman rate in 1972. The replacement rate for a human population is thought to be 2.1 children per woman, which means we are speedily closing in on stable, and then declining, population numbers, even if not as quickly as Weisman would like.

"Hurrah!" is the frequent reaction from the environmentally conscious, childfree or not. As we read bad news about global warming, poverty, diminishing resources, and so on, it seems that there are far too many people in the world and fewer of us would be a welcome development. But are there potential problems with depopulation? What is the societal and economic cost of fewer babies and more trees? And does it mean our duty to go forth and multiply should be renewed?

Here's where discussions of population growth become very complicated. The problem of global over-population competes with many individual nations' problem of depopulation. Nations like Italy and Japan, which have been experiencing depopulation for some time, are already conscious of the challenges it creates. As tax bases and labor pools decrease, schools close their doors and retirees worry about their pensions. However, in America, with a somewhat sustainable birthrate of 2.0, we hear far less about the potential shrinking markets, smaller tax bases, and diminishing labor pools. Yet even with a fertility rate of 2.0, America, like many of its European and Asian counterparts, is a graying nation. As sixty million baby boomers head for retirement, questions arise. Who will occupy our new houses? Who will work in our office buildings and tend our stores? Who will be paying into Social Security and Medicare? Many of us are under the false impression that we are paying into our own Social Security, when really we are paying for the benefits of the current retirees. A pay-as-you-go system worked fine in 1950 when there were more than seven workers for every one retiree, but today we are down to about four workers per retiree, and that number is estimated to dip under three to one by 2050. (10) We will be faced with the economic strain produced by the disparity in population size, but countries currently experiencing population loss are already looking for solutions. As in America, many modern nations have turned to immigration to fill the population gap. But in nations less accustomed to massive immigration, some have found that option triggers some ugly problems.

For example, Germany's birthrate of 1.3 is one of the lowest on the planet. This has led to a diminishing number of Germans and has played on the xenophobia of a small but vocal segment of society. Due to a huge gap in the labor pool, in 2000 the government issued twenty thousand work visas to qualified Indians badly needed for vacant high-tech jobs. In a 2000 election in the German state of North Rhine-Westphalia, the candidate for the Christian Democratic Union (CDU), Jürgen Rüttgers, coined the slogan "Kinder Statt Inder," or "Children not Indians." Happily, he was forced to remove the slogan amid protests from his more clearheaded countrypeople but the slogan still represents the sentiments of an enduring segment of society. The blatant racism is evidenced by the fact that newborns are no better at fixing computer networks than their parents are, and by the obvious fact that more babies means fewer German women in the workforce, thus increasing the gap in the labor pool, not shoring it up. Rüttgers lost the 2000 election but won in 2005. He is now the minister-president of his state and enjoys the support of the current prime minister, fellow CDU member Angela Merkel. These types of issues will continue to rear their ugly heads as cultures bump into each other at record speeds.

I like to think that in the U.S. we are more accustomed to different races mixing, even with the ever-present and growing backlash against Mexicans and Central Americans who are the backbone of the economy and the target for much disdain. That 2.0 birthrate that stabilizes our population, thus warding off some of the problems inherent in graying nations like Germany or Japan, is largely due to immigration, legal and otherwise, from places like Mexico. So, then, shall natural-born Americans and Europeans go forth and multiply in order to keep those markets booming, that tax base increasing, and those xenophobes comfy? Of course not.

It is hard to ignore the fact that a decreasing population may present some short-term economic effects and the even less sexy rise in racism. However, pushing for increased fertility rates as a way of growing the economy—black, white, brown, or whatever—is not a strategy for survival. Eventually, be it in ten years, a hundred years, or a thousand years, we would max out on elbow room and resources. The point may be moot, since most demographers agree that given current trends, it is highly unlikely that there will be a big turnaround in slowing global fertility rates anytime soon. As nations develop, healthcare improves and economic opportunity shifts from agricultural to industrial and/ or informational, fertility rates around the world continue to decrease. Other solutions will have to be found to the economic strain of aging populations and the social challenges of immigration.

Ellie, thirty-eight, would get us started by reining in all the waste. *"I don't buy into the idea that you have to have more people to support us as we age. We should be able to have fewer people supporting more people if the money is managed properly. The problem is that so much of it is wasted at a higher level of government. What about all of the billions of dollars spent in Iraq? How many people could that support? The claim that we have to have more kids so they can work some minimum wage jobs and pay taxes to support us when we are older is ludicrous. We just have to spend smarter, that's all."*

As other nations react to the inherent challenges of a declining birthrate, there's an opportunity to learn from them what works and what doesn't work. Two nations actively seeking to remedy the problem of declining birthrates are Germany and Italy, with their 1.3-children-per-woman fertility rates. In a 2008 *New York Times Magazine* article titled "No Babies?" Russell Shorto looks at the decline of Europe's fertility rate and strategies for coping with it. Many European states have implemented pro-natal programs that offer incentives and tax breaks to mothers. However, in the city of Laviano, Italy, the mayor actually offered a cash incentive equal to fifteen thousand dollars for each baby born. The result was an extremely small blip up in fertility and an extremely strained coffer that was not going to be able to maintain such a program for long. The majority of the cash recipients were already planning to have children, so rather than increasing fertility the program ended up paying lots of money for what it would have gotten anyway. (11)

While the urgency of making more German babies is a popular platform for some leaders, as was seen with Rüttgers, there are other, more inventive strategies also being implemented, with fantastic results. A consortium of seventeen cities in the former East German province of Saxony-Anhalt initiated a plan to constructively shrink in order to grow. Tearing down unused buildings and empty housing and replenishing the natural habitats on the land has created jobs and made the urban areas more alive while surrounding them in natural splendor. Rather than panicking and trying to bribe women into making babies, the consortium saw an opportunity to embrace the inevitable population decline and redesign cities for a healthy, sustainable future. (12)

In his book *The Empty Cradle*, Phillip Longman takes on the subject of declining birthrates and what to do about them from this socioeconomic perspective. He says: "Properly managed, the vast demographic transition now affecting nearly every corner of the globe could lead to a new era of stability and prosperity, as well as cultural and political maturity, particularly in regions where birthrates are falling and the labor force is still growing. Yet the examples to date of how rapidly aging societies are responding, or failing to respond, to the challenges that await them are hardly encouraging." Longman's suggestions for managing depopulation make good sense. He proposes ideas like home-based businesses, where children would once again be an asset rather than a liability. He envisions a shift back toward community-based economies, and sees no way the megalomania of big-box retailers and fast-food chains can endure. Like the innovative approaches in East Germany, Longman's ideas offer a vision of a different type of prosperity contingent on humanity's ability to acclimate to new demographics.

Germans and Italians aren't the only ones whose politicians complain about the lack of countrymen. On September 12, 2007 officials of the Russian government attempted to boost their sagging birthrate of 1.4 by instituting a "Conception Day." Nine months prior to Russia's national day of June 12, Conception Day is a contest to create a "patriot" to be born on the nation's holiday. Russians are given time off work for the purposes of "getting busy" on their entry, which can bring big prizes, like SUVs, electronics, and even cold hard cash. "The McLaughlin Group," a weekly show on PBS, discussed the merits, or lack thereof, of Conception Day. *Washington Times* conservative columnist Tony Blankley argued: "The problem of not having babies isn't the failure to have sex, it's the failure to have enough sense of contributing to your society to want to have children." (13)

It is precisely this type of belief system that the childfree have to defend themselves against. The idea that having children means you care about society and not having them means you don't couldn't be more false. Arguably, the greatest contribution we childfrees make, whether intentionally or by happy accident, is saving the planet from further exploitation by another ravenous consumer. There is a great opportunity for modern nations to lead the way to healthy sustainability for all of earth's inhabitants, be they two-legged, four-legged, winged, or finned. If our national identities and economies are dependent on population growth, then it is those concepts that need to be reexamined and redefined. At the moment, the majority of the depopulation rhetoric is geared toward figuring out why we brazen childfree women are intent on destroying society and how we can be lured into reproducing, rather than seeing this as a development necessary for everyone's survival. If depopulation has some short-term negatives, then we should be listening to new ideas like those of Longman, and finding ways to adapt as people in East Germany are doing, not pushing for more babies.

BLAME A FEMINIST

What is good for our planet may not be so good for our pocketbooks, which makes me wonder: if we continue on our current path of population decline and the outcome is negative, economically or socially, who will we get to blame? Will it be ineffective politicians' failure to lead? Materialism and greed run amok in a society unwilling to change its lifestyle? Maybe, but my guess is that childfree women will be left holding the bag. Some social and religious conservatives have already pointed an accusatory finger our way.

In his anti-immigration, not-so-subtly-racist book, *The Death of the West,* Patrick J. Buchanan explains that birthrates among Europeans and Americans of European descent (meaning the white folk) are well below the replacement rate of 2.1. By page 39 he is already blaming overeducated feminists who wanted to enter the world of work and gain their independence, thus destroying a family-oriented society. (14)

One imperative that was lost, he claims, was the "family wage," wherein it was perfectly legal to pay a man a higher wage than a woman, because, after all, he had a family to support. The man may or may not have had a family to support, but he still benefited from higher wages. Conversely, women who were working in the few positions available to them (teacher, nurse, secretary, librarian, etc.) made about half of a man's wage. Their income was, after all, supplemental. The problem, however, was not that angry feminists conspired to destroy America, but that in the 1950s one in four marriages ended in divorce, and by the late 1960s the divorce rate was already one in three, resulting in huge numbers of single-mother households. (15) These invisible, ignored, even scorned members of society were often raising children alone because their men had failed them, and thus they lived with their children in poverty. Child support enforcement was virtually nonexistent, so it was a roll of the dice whether or not there would be any income coming in. Even if single mothers could scrape together a couple of bucks, forget about getting a mortgage. Women in the late 1960s were not granted credit unless they were married and the account was in their husband's name. Women were dependent on men for security, wealth, and social status. When they were abandoned with their children, they turned to the free society they lived in to try and make their way. The problem was, the classified ads had only two sections—high-paying jobs for men and low-paying jobs for women. There were no "single, head of household" job listings, and women and children suffered as a result. So, if conservative pundits like Pat Buchanan wonder why by the 1960s women seemed so angry, that was part of it. But where is the book about how men failed the family, leaving women and children to fend for themselves? Only by yelling, shouting, demonstrating, and becoming radical did women get gender added to the list of things not to be discriminated against in the workplace. In 1963, the equal pay for equal work amendment was added to the Fair Labor Standards Act, leading the way to emancipation. While almost fifty years later women still make seventy-seven cents on the dollar compared to what their male counterparts earn, they're a lot better off than they were in 1963. God bless the feminists.

Today, with a divorce rate of almost one in two (16), it is rare that a woman has children without considering the possibility of one day being a single mom. According to the U.S. Census Bureau, as of 2007 84% of single, custodial parents were women. Many of the women I talked to for this book cited that fear as a big deterrent to childbearing. Some of them were raised by single moms and watched the struggles live and in person. Others were raised in intact families, but the toils of single moms were not lost on them as they watched friends and neighbors suffer. Even women I encounter who desperately want to be mothers cite the fear of being a single mom as one reason for their hesitation. Can they find an emotionally and financially stable enough partner to raise a family with in this day and age? There are certainly no guarantees.

Karen, thirty-five, studied women's studies and human sexuality in school. "*My biggest fear was to get into a relationship with someone, have a family, and then have them leave. My thought was more that I would be the one who got stuck with custody, not the one who would want custody. I saw that as such a negative, which furthered my belief that I shouldn't have children."*

Natalie is thirty-one and was seven years old when her parents divorced. She has been happily married for three years, but knows the score. *"When it comes to having children, men really do tend to get off easy. If there is a divorce, they're able to move out and do their own thing, but women can't. A single dad is a really remarkable thing, while single mothers are everywhere."*

The plight of the single mom is one of many complicated issues that fuel the feminist movement to this day. We will take a closer look at this plight in the next chapter; however, post–women's liberation, there are still countless single mothers living in poverty with their children. Even though these women are working and raising the next generation of Americans, they continue to endure low social status. Single fathers, on the other hand, are revered and praised like saints. Women who leave their husbands and children are seen as pariahs, while fathers who do the same simply move on. These dads, who are often estranged from their kids within a few years, experience almost no social stigma at all. It is easy to blame a feminist for the decline of the American family, but we couldn't have millions of single mothers without millions of men who failed to live up to their end of the family responsibility too.

Pat Buchanan is right about one thing—since the women's movement the birthrate has gone down. While some, like Buchanan, may argue that we are birth-controlling ourselves out of existence in the West, there is no way that the planet can support an unlimited number of people, either. With a net gain of seventy-seven million folks each year, it would be wiser to look at why fertility rates in the West are declining and advocate similar trends in other nations. It is easy for us in America to forget that whether or not to have children is not a personal choice available to women—or men, for that matter—in much of the world. Higher education, access to birth control, gender equality, and economic opportunity are all leading to lower birthrates in many developing nations. Supporting such trends around the world while preparing for the changes brought about by depopulation is the path to sustainable living for all. But the fight to deny women the education and the means to prevent unwanted pregnancy continues to be waged by the faithfully inspired yet factually challenged religious right.

IGNORANCE-ONLY EDUCATION

For eons, religious zealots have been trying to tell everyone else what to do, how to think, how to behave, and so on. They are very good at pointing out the splinter in someone else's eye while ignoring the giant log in their own. Everything from torture, to slavery, to the subjugation of women, to the suppression of birth control and sex education has been justified in the name of God. Because churches always need new members, and kids make great recruits, there's not a lot of support for the childfree life coming from the pulpit. For childfrees raised under strict religious rule, gaining acceptance can be a challenge. That was something Shannon, thirty-five, had to get beyond. *"I grew up in a very conservative, evangelical church environment where women were not allowed to wear anything but* *dresses or skirts; we weren't allowed to listen to any music with a drumbeat; we didn't go to movie theaters because they also showed R-rated movies; and my parents took away my Barbie dolls because they were worldly. When I was about twenty-five, my grandmother and I had a conversation where she said, 'How do you know what God's plans are for you? Maybe it is to have children.' I was not as confident or as outspoken about my decision to be childfree then, so I didn't really have much of a response. But today I do have a response, which is, 'How do you know that God's plan for me isn't **not** to be a mother?' I certainly can't tell you what God means for you to do, and vice versa."*

Luckily for Shannon, even though she grew up in an Evangelical household, the option of birth control was in her awareness and she eventually had her tubes tied. These days, the religious right works very hard at keeping our youth ignorant of the workings of their own bodies.

If ever a more cunning, manipulative, and downright dishonest attempt at controlling sexuality and reproduction than "abstinence-only sex education" was thrust on American youth, I haven't seen it. Although started in 1996 under Clinton, with his propensity to bend to the Republican Congress of the day, it really took off with Bush in 2001. With the beginning of Bush's administration, the only schools eligible for the 170 million federal tax dollars available each year for sex education had to agree to adhere exclusively to the abstinence-only curriculum, despite the lack of efficacy studies. Right off the bat I must point out that abstinence-only-until-marriage programs, all of which are forbidden to discuss birth control methods unless it is to point out their failure rates, assumes that after marriage there is no need to know how to prevent pregnancy. This offends me to my very core. The assumption that all married people welcome children is obviously false or I wouldn't be writing this book. Even married people who want children generally don't want an unlimited number. But the absence of information on pregnancy prevention as a matter of factual, human biology is just the beginning of the failure. Not only were these programs completely untested when implemented, but a 2004 report from the Congressional Oversight and Reform Committee showed that over 80 percent of the curriculum contained false and/or misleading statements. (17) Parents, 90 percent of whom believe accurate reproductive information should be taught in schools, should be outraged by the outlandish claims contained in these programs.

For example, one program states that the Institute of Medicine has found a connection between chlamydia and heart attacks. However, the research cited actually showed that the bacterium known as *Chlamydia pneumoniae,* which is spread through respiratory transmission, was linked to heart attacks—not the bacterium *Chlamydia trachomatis,* which is a sexually transmitted infection (STI). Another curriculum states that 5 percent to 10 percent of women who undergo legal abortions will become sterile, and that premature birth and tubal and cervical pregnancies increase following abortions. In fact, there is no evidence that these risks increase after the procedure used in most abortions in the United States. As for condom usage, many of the abstinence-only programs hail one scientific study done in 1993 by Dr. Susan Weller that concluded that condoms were effective in reducing HIV/AIDS transmissions by only 69 percent. (18) This study was rejected by the Department of Health and Human Services in 1997 because of serious methodological problems. (19) In addition, countless studies have been done over the years demonstrating time and time again that—when used correctly—condoms are 98–100 percent effective in preventing both disease and pregnancy. Obviously, when used incorrectly or inconsistently, efficacy rates will go down. The Centers for Disease Control and Prevention weighed in on its Web site, www.cdc.gov, stating:

Latex condoms, when used consistently and correctly, are highly effective in preventing transmission of HIV, the virus that causes AIDS. In addition, correct and consistent use of latex condoms can reduce the risk of other sexually transmitted diseases (STDs), including discharge and genital ulcer diseases. While the effect of condoms in preventing human papillomavirus (HPV) infection is unknown, condom use has been associated with a lower rate of cervical cancer, an HPV-associated disease.

In practice, when human error and inconsistency are factored in, condom failure rates are about 15 percent. According to the World Health Organization, the difference between typical and perfect use "is due primarily to inconsistent and incorrect use, not to condom failure. Condom failure—the device breaking or slipping off during intercourse—is uncommon." HBO's Bill Maher summed it up beautifully by saying, "I have been using these things for thirty-five years. I've never had one condom break. Either

I'm the luckiest son of a bitch who ever was (and I'm not!) or this is the most reliable product since the toaster!" (20)

If we know for sure that they work best when used correctly and consistently, it would stand to reason that some training is in order. Unfortunately, the research shows that kids schooled in abstinence-only sex education who had taken the subsequent "virginity pledge" were just as likely to engage in premarital sex as their counterparts, but have fewer sexual partners and are *less likely* to use condoms or any other contraceptive. (21) As a result, their rate of STDs is about the same as that of their non-pledging peers. Another disturbing finding is that pledge takers may be more likely to engage in other risky behaviors in lieu of intercourse, such as oral and anal sex, than non-pledgers. (22)

But the leaders of this movement are undeterred. "We teach abstinence because it's the truth; we don't analyze ourselves based on reducing the risk," says Denny Pattyn, founder of Silver Ring Thing (23), an evangelical group that received federal funding. Well, there you have it, folks, the so-called Christian protectors of our youth would rather see kids get sick than teach them accurate sex information.

These pointless attempts at controlling sexual behavior are not only unethical, but also appear to be reversing a fifteen-year trend of steadily declining teen pregnancy rates. One of our great social success stories is being obliterated under the false promise of a public policy that is dishonest and obviously ineffectual.

In 2006, the United States saw a notable spike in fertility rates, jumping from 2.0 to 2.1. (24) While the increase in birthrates was seen across the board for

American women, the increase in teenage births is most alarming. Between the years of 1991 and 2005, teenage motherhood declined by 34 percent in this country, a statistic well worth celebrating. However, from 2005 to 2006, the teen birthrate rose an alarming 3 percent. (25) It is still too soon to determine a definitive cause, but there are already theories floating around about the failure of abstinence-only education and increasingly difficult access to both birth control and abortion.

In order to continue promoting their agenda, the religious right tells brazen lies to America's youth, putting them at risk for unplanned parenthood and disease. They want to get those babies here by any means necessary, even if it's trickery. Unlike abstinence-only programs, comprehensive sex education does have a proven track record of reducing risky sexual behavior in teens. The American Psychological Association stated, "Based on over 15 years of research, the evidence shows that comprehensive sexuality education programs for youth that encourage abstinence, promote appropriate condom use, and teach sexual communication skills reduce HIV-risk behavior and also delay the onset of sexual intercourse." (26)

Abstinence-only sex education is one of the flagship programs of the pro-life crowd. However, it has become increasingly obvious that the pro-life movement is not pro-life, but pro-birth. As stated by progressive evangelical leader Jim Wallis, "If I'm an unborn child and I want the support of the far religious right I better stay unborn as long as possible because once I'm born I'm off the radar screen. No health care, no child care, no education, no nothing."

So, as long as the "pro-birth" movement of the religious right continues to focus single-mindedly on bringing babies into being, wanted or not, we will continue to see fear tactics, falsehoods, and fabrications in its teachings. Nothing could be less pro-child, pro-family, or pro-life.

But with a relatively new administration in Washington, we have a chance to correct this travesty thrust upon our youth. Over the last decade, more than 1.5 billion federal tax dollars went to ineffectual and inaccurate abstinence-only programs (27), while zero dollars went toward proven comprehensive sex education. However, President Obama's 2010 budget cancelled all abstinence-only funding, leaving those determined to continue the abstinence-only sham scrambling for private funding that is unlikely to fill the massive shortfall.

Most childfrees whom I have talked to, along with many parents, I am sure, see the intentional misinformation being given to kids as extremely undemocratic. Thomas Jefferson said, "If a nation expects to be ignorant and free in a state of civilization, it expects what never was and never will be." In the face of overwhelming data on the failure of abstinence-only programs, many states didn't wait for a federal change; instead, they opted out of the federal funds. The only state on the ball enough to reject the funds from the get-go, California, was joined by Pennsylvania in 2004 and Maine in 2005. However, the ranks grew by thirteen additional states in 2007, and was up to twenty-two by the end of 2009. (28) It is encouraging to see a return to truth and reason. Only an educated, well-informed population can rule itself. Therefore, accurate information on health and reproduction should be taught and easily accessible to all.

We know that the human race is putting a huge strain on our planet. Only by living in balance with the natural world can we really be "pro-life." Reducing population, not growing it, is the only "pro-life" position that makes any sense. We should be supporting solid family planning both here and abroad, while seeking workable solutions to the social and economic problems we could encounter as a result. Instead, we have allowed our schools to lie to children, and have supported a government that has exported those lies around the world.

The highest fertility rate on the planet is in sub-Saharan Africa, at about 5.1; largely due to HIV/AIDS, they have the highest death rates as well. (29) Ignoring the fact that 5 percent of adults age fifteen to forty-nine in sub-Saharan Africa are living with HIV/AIDS, and regardless of the reality that 1.6 million of the 2.1 million AIDS deaths in 2007 were in sub-Saharan Africa, and even though that continent has over twelve million AIDS orphans (30), and despite the lack of evidence of any abstinence-only sex education program having any efficacy whatsoever, the former Bush administration exported these failed programs abroad, costing Americans billions in tax dollars and denying Africans lifesaving information. How did an administration that claimed to be "pro-life" justify backing such an insidious policy, fueling the flames of a widespread pandemic that has devastated families by the millions?

In 2003, then President Bush passed the President's Emergency Plan for AIDS Relief (PEPFAR), allocating fifteen billion dollars over five years to fight the disease. While even some of the most outspoken AIDS activists, like U2 lead singer Bono, applauded the bill, it turned out that there was a big, fat earmark for abstinence-only programs. The bill required that in order to receive funds, a minimum of one-third of the money designated for AIDS *prevention* must go to abstinence-only programs. This was a travesty for the women, who have little or no control over their sexual lives. Beatrice Were, the founder of Uganda's National Community of Women Living with HIV and AIDS, said in July 2005, "We are expected to abstain when we are young girls and to be faithful when we are married to men who rape us, who are not necessarily faithful to us, who batter us."

Few men in sub-Saharan Africa are faithful to one sexual partner, while their wives have no authority to refuse their philandering husbands or to negotiate condom use, thereby making marriage one of the biggest risk factors for women of the region. In fact, an estimated 60–80 percent of HIV-positive women were infected by their husbands, who were their sole partners. (31) In addition, the U.S. government's own oversight report shows that in order to hit funding requirements for abstinence-only programs, crucial resources for other prevention programs, such as mother-to-child infection prevention, were cut. (32) In areas like rural South Africa and Swaziland, where an estimated 50 percent of pregnant women are HIV-positive, the unproven, ideological requirements of the Bush administration were a death sentence for untold numbers of newborns. This part of American foreign policy ignored the cultural realities of women in Africa, and mothers and babies have paid with their lives.

In early 2008, President Bush traveled to Africa to tout his one success as leader of the free world and grasp at a legacy for himself. In usual form, the American media jumped on the bandwagon, megaphoning this triumph throughout the land. By pumping up the many successes of the program, the Bush administration tried to pressure Congress for a quick and tidy reauthorization of PEPFAR. Not so fast, George. In April 2008, the now Democratic Congress did reauthorize PEPFAR, but increased funding from thirty billion dollars to fifty billion dollars and removed the abstinence-only requirement. That requirement was replaced by a far more sensible policy of balanced funding for abstinence, fidelity, and condom programs based on evidence for each target country, truly a lifesaving "pro-life" shift in direction.

Given the multitude of social, economic, and health issues facing the 6.8 billion people already here on planet Earth, the obsession with creating more of us eludes the childfree. I am grateful that I live in a place where this is my choice to make, and I am making it. Once the same social and economic advantages that women of the developed world enjoy are available to women across the globe, we will see lower birthrates, better health, and less poverty, and we will enjoy a more sustainable environment.

BIRTH CONTROL BATTLES

American Teenagers and Africans are not the only ones who struggle with birth control issues, however. While the availability of safe and legal abortion is the one failsafe that guarantees a woman the choice of being childfree, it is not seen as a means to rely on by any of the people I spoke with. Good thing, since in late 2009 yet another abortion fight was surfacing on

Capitol Hill. The healthcare reform debate heated up when the Democrat-controlled House of Representatives finally passed their version of a bill with a last-minute amendment that restricted the coverage of abortion by any insurer who wanted to participate in the newly proposed insurance exchange program. Pro-choice women have long relied on the Democratic Party to fight for their reproductive rights. Yet the proposed Stupak Amendment was added by *Democratic* Representative Bart Stupak of Michigan, signaling the end of that reliance and reminding all women that governance over their own bodies is in serious jeopardy. The Stupak Amendment was replaced in the final bill with language that restricts the use of federal money for elective abortions but doesn't necessarily ban private insurers from covering them. The fact that both the Stupak Amendment and subsequent compromise were both written by Democrats and passed by a Democrat-controlled congress shows how very vulnerable pro-choice women are.

Because the childfree have given deep thought to their decision not to have children, pregnancy prevention is a duty taken quite seriously for those in heterosexual relationships. Some have even elected to undergo sterilization procedures, thus permanently closing the door on reproduction. While their reasons for undergoing these procedures are similar, childfrees' experiences in obtaining sterilization vary greatly. While just about anyone who has had a couple of kids can obtain permanent sterilization without much hassle, it can be difficult to find a doctor willing to perform the operation on a childfree. The prevailing wisdom seems to be that deciding to have children requires no reflection but deciding not to requires a referral for counseling.

Meagn, now forty-nine years old, explains, *"When I was twenty years old I walked into the gynecologist's office and said I wanted to have a tubal ligation, and he looked at me like I was crazy. He said it would be okay if I had already had two children, but given my age and the fact that I didn't have children, it was going to be a big problem. It wasn't until six years later that I finally talked a doctor into doing it. He said at age twenty-six that I was too young to have the procedure, but finally I said, 'If I came in here and told you I wanted to have a baby, would you tell me I was too young?' That convinced him, and I got my tubal ligation. I was really glad to get it, because in the early eighties I could feel the cold breath of a coming theocracy on the back of my neck, and I thought,* The day is going to come when this is going to be prohibited. *I'm really glad I haven't been proven right—yet!"*

Concern over losing the right to choose prompted Karen, now thirty-five, to have tubal ligation at age twenty-nine. She had to go through several doctors, but finally found one who would do it. *"I had to write a letter explaining that I understood the surgery and that it was permanent. Then the doctor still had to do a bunch of counseling with me before finally agreeing to do it. I got asked things like, 'What will you do if you change your mind?' or 'What if you meet somebody who wants a family?' No one asks someone who wants children or who is pregnant, 'What if you meet someone who doesn't want a family? What if you change your mind after having the baby?' But the thing that really prompted me to find a doctor who would do the surgery was the aftermath of September eleventh. My thought was that if this president can take away so many civil rights, it's only a matter of time before abortion and all the other reproductive rights are gone. Since*

I never wanted to have children, I never wanted to be faced with an unplanned pregnancy. So while it was still possible, I decided, I'm going to do this. "

The childfree are overwhelmingly pro-choice, but because they are deliberately choosing not to have kids, they take responsibility for preventing pregnancy. Whether their birth control method is permanent or not, those who need it always use a medically sound method. To someone who is not childfree, the hesitancy of a doctor to perform sterilization on a woman who is twenty, twenty-six, or even twenty-nine years old who has not borne children may be understandable. To the childfree, it is offensive and ridiculous. When women of that age go to a doctor for help getting pregnant, they are never counseled on the seriousness of such a decision. When has a doctor ever reminded a potential mother, "You do know that having a baby is permanent? We cannot reverse it once it is done." However, even today, women can still run into scorn and judgment simply for seeking birth control to prevent an unwanted pregnancy.

Kristen, forty-two, and Scott, forty-one, have been married for twenty years and are very comfortable with their decision to be childfree. However, Kristen's doctor wasn't so sure. *"I had a gynecologist once who wouldn't prescribe me birth control because, according to her, I was at the age where I should be having children. She asked me why I didn't have children, and I explained I didn't want them, but she wouldn't let it go. She kept asking why, so I said I didn't have the patience. She just said patience would come in time. She really couldn't comprehend that I didn't want any children. So I started getting mad and said, 'Do you understand that this is my choice, not yours?' After I left there, I wrote her a letter saying how wrong she was. Who is she to tell me what to do? How dare she impose her opinions on me? You can be sure, that was the last time I ever saw that doctor."*

The debates about overpopulation, declining birthrates, sex education, sexual mores, and STDs are far from over. If economic prosperity continues to be dependent on population growth, then as populations decline to a more sustainable level we will be forced to adapt and find new ways to meet our survival needs. Meanwhile, women of all nationalities should be free to make reproductive choices based on what is best for them, their families, their circumstances, and the greater good. Perhaps some of us—brazen, childless women that we are—will be the ones who solve this population dilemma, ending poverty, stopping AIDS, and creating sustainable living for us all. With more of us educated, active, and participating politically and socially, it is not so far-fetched.

4

The Fastest Way to End a First Date...or Find Your Mate!

Although there are many trial marriages...there is no such thing as a trial child.

—Gail Sheehy

They sit down at the table, cautiously sizing each other up. First dates are always such an exercise in awkwardness. After drinks and appetizers, things start to relax a bit. The conversation is flowing, and there is clearly a spark of attraction. So far, so good. Subjects covered up to this point include: work, weather, hometowns, and so on. Then, after the second round of drinks is served, they start getting into the good stuff: "How long have you been single?" "What was your ex like?" And then, here comes the doozy: "Why didn't it work out?" The childfree single's heart drops. Is it time for truth or consequences already?

Truth: "He wanted to have children, and I did not. We couldn't agree on a compromise." She holds her breath, waiting for a reply. Could this be the one? Could he actually say, "I don't want to have kids, either!"—or will she watch as the smile fades, the eyes grow cold, and the conversation turns back to surface issues as they go through the motions, finish the date, and say good night and good-bye forever? It is a risky proposition. Why not save that conversation for another day? Why waste all this good chemistry? She could just as easily reply, "We wanted different things; we were headed in different directions." Isn't that still true? Or at least true-ish? But then come the...

Consequences: Fast-forward to three months later. A harmless little tryst is quickly becoming a serious relationship with some long-term potential. Genuine feelings are starting to develop. Hearts are on the line as vulnerability comes into play. Then one Saturday afternoon the new couple is strolling through the park, surrounded by the laughter of children on the playground, and he looks lovingly into her eyes and says, "Wouldn't it be great to have a family one day?" Ugh. Now she's in trouble. And she's not the only one. According to the U.S. Census, over five million women between the ages of fifteen and forty-four declare themselves voluntarily childless. (1) However, as one researcher noted, the number may actually be higher due to the reluctance to be public about it. Voluntarily childless men are not counted by the census, however it is a pretty safe bet that at least as many men would identify that way as women. That makes over 10 million childless by choice adults out there building lives and forming relationships, just like everyone else.

CAN'T WE JUST COMPROMISE?

How childfree singles approach the dating scene may vary, but one thing remains true. At some point the truth is going to come out. Once a couple has developed genuine feelings for each other, walking away gets a lot harder. Desperate attempts to find a solution may be proposed. How about only one child? What if they adopted? Maybe he could be happy without kids? If they love each other, they should be able to figure this out. Don't all relationships require give-and-take?

Vicki, forty-six, was upfront as early as possible, but a few times still wound up involved with men who wanted kids. *"In the past I have broken things off with guys who wanted kids, and when they would ask why, I would say, 'It's not fair for me to pursue a relationship with someone who wants children when I know that I don't. Better to end it now than to have really hurt feelings later down the road.' Then I met my husband, and from our first lunch date I just knew that I had waited for a reason. He was the one."*

Ask any committed couple with some longevity under their belts about the secrets to a successful relationship, and you are guaranteed to find "compromise" up there near the top of the list. The ability to travel through life for twenty, thirty, forty, fifty years or more with one primary person at your side will most certainly require lots of that. So what does compromise really mean? Let's check with Webster's:

Compromise – (kom'prə miz') n., v., -n 1. a settlement of differences by *mutual adjustment* **or modification of opposing claims, principles, demands, etc.; agreement by mutual concession. 2. the result of such a settlement. 3. something** *intermediate between* **different things.** [Emphasis added]

The words that jump off the page are "mutual," "intermediate," and "between." One has to wonder, then, whether or not a couple can "compromise" on the issue of children. If a compromise is an intermediate point between two positions, where is the halfway point between having kids and not? Answer: There is none! We can't have a little bit of kids or have kids for a while and then give them back. It is a binary code situation. One or zero. Yes or no. On or off. Do or don't. There is no compromise.

As a minister, Kathleen gets to talk to couples a lot about their plans to have or not to have kids. *"I do pre-marital counseling with lots of couples. My red flag goes up when I ask them if they are going to have kids and the answer is, 'We're not sure; we're going to see what happens.' I definitely want to go further with that. I ask if they are both unsure, if one is less sure than the other, etc. It can really be a deal breaker later on if a couple is not on the same page with that."*

Andrea and her husband were married for four years and together for ten. When the kid issue came up they tried the counseling route. *"Back then, I was saying, 'I don't think I want to have kids' rather than 'I don't want to have kids' because I wasn't sure how to say it. So we actually went to a counselor to talk about it. She said things like, 'You love animals, so I'm sure you'll change your mind.' It was really all about mind changing, rather than exploring the issues. It was very strange. We had a lot of other issues, too, so our disagreement about having kids became something to blame everything on and we eventually split up."*

Ellie, thirty-eight, has a friend going through that very struggle right now. *"A couple we're friends with have both always said they're not having kids, but now in their mid-thirties he is starting to say he might want them after all. This is a big red flag for her, and she is really stressed about it. I don't know if they will be able to find a solution. You really can't compromise when it is your body; you will have to birth it, breastfeed it, and, if the relationship fails, you're stuck with it."*

Eileen, forty-eight, is single and dating. She has always been upfront about her decision not to have children, and has even left relationships because of it. Currently she is dating a man much younger than she is, and at thirty-five he is starting to rethink his decision. *"When we first started dating I was very clear that I didn't want to have children, and he was okay with that. But recently he lost his mother to lung cancer, and it's been devastating for him. Somehow, this has led to the kid issue coming up again. He said to me, 'I always thought I would have the option of whether or not to have kids.' Because he is still so raw from the loss of his mother, we decided to table the issue and give him some time to heal. However, very soon we'll have to sit down and have that discussion again. If it's something that he wants in his life, I certainly don't want to deny him that. It makes me very sad and it would be hard to walk away, but I would. Fact is, it's a no-compromise issue."*

Karen, thirty-five, now lives with her childfree boyfriend, but she has been there. *"In one serious relationship I had, it came up on the first date. He said things like, 'When I have kids, I think I want to buy them two of each toy and let them play with one and save one so I can bring it out when they're more grown-up.' My response was to say that I didn't want to have kids, and even though that was something he always wanted he entered the relationship anyhow. We had very different ideas about the future. He wanted to settle down, get married, and have kids, and he knew that wasn't an option for me, but he was still with me. We dated almost two years, but after a while we couldn't move forward anymore. There was no way to compromise."*

In a relationship in which one partner wants children and the other does not, "compromise" takes on a whole new meaning. Instead of mutually adjusting to an intermediate point between the two, in this case, one person gives in and the other person gets his or her way. This is a concession, not a compromise, and can have devastating results. Many childfree singles have found out the hard way that their childfree status adds yet another confusing element to the complicated world of dating.

Now married for five years, Lori, forty-three, had to learn the hard way what happens when you date people who want to parent. *"When I was twenty I had my first serious relationship, but he wanted kids and I didn't. That was the reason we broke up. Several years later I had another serious relationship where I was actually engaged. He knew I didn't want to have kids, but finally admitted that he always thought I would change my mind, so that relationship ended. Foolishly, I got back together with him a few years later, and lo and behold the same issue came up again. A month later it was over for good."*

When dating casually, telling someone you don't want to have children from the get-go may feel presumptuous, while keeping that bit of info under your hat may feel misleading. But don't look for a childfree dating guide at your local bookseller. The countless dating books found lining the shelves address one goal, and that is landing the future father of your children, by any manipulative means necessary. For example, Ellen Fein and Sherrie Schneider warn us in *The Rules: Time-tested Secrets for Capturing the Heart of Mr. Right* never to mention words like **marriage**, **wedding**, **children**, or **future** in any context whatsoever: "those are subjects for him to bring up." (2) Thus, they advise women to give up all of their power and become wimpy little waifs. They go on to advise women to downplay their accomplishments, letting him be the one who shines. So if you are looking for an egomaniac or commitment-phobe to have a litter with, you should do great. If those rules seem a bit phony or manipulative, fear not. The book later assures readers that once he says, "I love you," you can be more yourself.

Manipulative, chauvinistic advice like that found in *The Rules* may appeal to someone on a mission for the mythical holy grail of happy endings—marriage and baby. The rest of us have to figure out our own rules.

Because families, culture, and/or society put so much pressure on women to get married and have babies, many find themselves hitched long before being able to fully explore their personal truth about parenting. Stacey is thirty-eight and has been married to her second husband for five years; however, it took a moment of truth in her first marriage to really solidify her desire to remain childfree. *"My first husband really wanted to have kids. Actually, he really wanted to be a grandfather, and if he could have skipped right to that part, he would've! I started thinking perhaps I could do it; after all, everyone always told me I'd be a great mother. He was really pushing it, but at the same time my mom got really ill and I knew there was just no way. I got to a point where I couldn't live in denial anymore; I couldn't deny it to myself or anyone else how I really felt about it. It really started to tear at my marriage, and after five years we split. That solidified it for me. His really wanting kids made me realize that I really didn't. I had deluded myself for a while, thinking that with the right kind of support and the right kind of help I could probably do it. But when push came to shove, I didn't want to."*

LOVE, MARRIAGE, BABY CARRIAGE

The belief that marriage and family are the ultimate happy ending is the conventional wisdom that supports the survival of our species. As we saw in chapter 1, the idea that children bring fulfillment to all endures in spite of overwhelming evidence to the contrary. Popular culture supports this misconception with endless television shows and movies that solve all human dramas with marriage and babies. No wonder so many accomplished women feel forever lacking unless they are coupled and/or breeding. I have known many wonderful women saddled with some lackluster guy simply because they have been taught there is some sort of redemption in coupledom. There isn't. But still, everywhere we look, we see examples of what it means to live happily ever after.

Even as mainstream America begins to change its attitudes about another subgroup in society, the gay and lesbian population, positive role models of the child-free life are still largely absent from popular culture. The NBC sitcom "Will & Grace" was considered a very a cutting-edge television show when it aired from 1998 to 2006. Based on a gay guy/straight girl friendship, the show broke new ground, demystifying and normalizing the gay lifestyle for many viewers. The success of the show demonstrated America's readiness to embrace the estimated 10 percent of our citizens who identify as homosexual into at least some public arenas. It is amazing that something as controversial as homosexuality has "come out of the closet" in popular culture, but the estimated 10 percent of childfree Americans still find themselves strangely invisible. Even in a breakthrough show like "Will & Grace," the series finale ends with Grace happily married to a doctor and mothering her little Lyla, while Will is coupled with his longtime love, Vince, and has adopted baby Ben. To add to the mythology, Lyla and Ben later meet at college, fall in love, and of course get married. Other popular shows, like "Friends" and "Frasier," overwhelmingly wrapped things up with happily-ever-afters for all. I am sure we all slept better knowing that Ross and Rachel got back together to raise their baby; Monica and Chandler were completed with adopted children; and Niles and Daphne finally walked down the aisle and she quickly became pregnant despite his low sperm count.

The undesirable status of being single, childless, and pushing forty is a stereotype that remains alive and well in these types of shows. Family comedies are chock-full of the unmarried side characters who are either too deranged or too pathetic to land a mate and pop out a baby. "Roseanne" had her single basket case of a sister, Jackie; "Still Standing" had the desperate sister-in-law, Linda; and "Everybody Loves Raymond" had Ray's brother Robert, divorced and living with their parents, to name a few. Even the show that was going to celebrate being over thirty and single, "Sex and the City," ended up more like a frantic quest for Mr. Right (or Mr. Big, as the case may be). The happy, well-adjusted singleton and/or childfree continues to be glaringly absent from prime time.

Then there are the books, or the so-called "chick lit." With so much popular fiction directed at women, it is no surprise that the same old "happy endings" wrap up novel after novel. When I picked up *Baby Proof* by Emily Giffin, I was hoping for a great story about a strong, self-assured, childfree woman who was not going to get hoodwinked into motherhood. The main character actually ended her marriage when her fellow childfree husband changed his mind. The whole time I was reading it, I kept thinking that if this ends with her having a baby and getting her man back I was going to be severely disappointed. I fought the urge to skip to the last page, but when I arrived there, I was relieved to find out that although she and her husband reconciled, at least he was okay again with not being a dad. I would have celebrated it in full, if it hadn't been for the main character's closing thoughts: "I don't know if I will ever overcome my fears of motherhood. Whether I will someday be a mother. Whether I am capable of being a good one." (4)

Fears? Oh, it was going so well, right up until the end. The assertion that her desire to be childfree was based on fear crushed what was otherwise a pretty decent beach read. So the search continues for positive childfree character role models.

But they won't be found in the movies. Two films that looked at the desire, or lack thereof, to parent, but ultimately disappointed were *Waitress* and *Juno*. *Waitress* is a romantic comedy about a poor waitress married to an abusive husband who finds herself unhappily pregnant with his child. She is trapped by her marriage and now trapped by the baby she has absolutely no feelings for—until the end, of course. After delivering the baby, she resists even looking at it, but once she lays eyes on the little screamer she is instantly transformed. In less than a minute, she has told off her husband, sent him packing, and fully embraced her new role as poverty-stricken single mother with a smile on her face. If that weren't bad enough, her magical transformation is miraculously rewarded when the old man she has been serving pie to all those months of pregnancy endows her with a gob of money to start her own pie shop! This ridiculous movie played right into the conventional wisdom that baby fixes all, ignoring the sad statistics about the realities of single motherhood covered later in this chapter.

Then we have the spunky little Juno. *Juno* is the story of a wisecracking pregnant teen and the yuppie couple chosen to adopt her unwanted spawn, as she refers to it. However, when the adoptive father has second thoughts and backs out of the deal, he is made out to be an overgrown adolescent who would rather pursue foolish dreams than raise a child. Instead of portraying him as an artist and musician willing to sacrifice security for the pursuit of his true passions, he is ensconced in creepiness with hints of an attraction to the pregnant teen. In *Juno* we are supposed to see the pregnant teen as responsible and the thirty-something man who is reconsidering the decision to be a parent as a flake. Go figure. Of course, the uptight wife who railroads him into fatherhood to begin with is never accused of selfishness, let alone neurosis. In fact, she still gets the baby in the end! Nice and tidy.

Like the prospective father in *Juno*, many adults consider having a child in order to save their marriage or relationship. But if you feel tempted to ignore your intuition and have a child merely to fit into the baby club, believing that everything will just "click," you are setting yourself up for a lifetime of disappointment. As we saw in chapter 1, the research actually shows that marital satisfaction decreases after the birth of a child. Instead of fixing things, this course of action is likely to amplify existing problems and only painfully prolong the inevitable. Be warned—having children to fix a rocky partnership is a tempting trap that will most likely result in single parenthood. One childfree I spoke with barely escaped exactly that fate.

Miriam is a forty-three-year-old musician and massage therapist who, like many women, grew up thinking she would have children "one day." *"When I was about twenty, I thought I wanted children. Not that I wanted them at twenty, but I thought I would want one at some point. As I got older, about twenty-five or so, it began to feel like a foolish thing to do. I wanted to pursue a career in music, and I didn't want to compromise that. It didn't come with enough money to afford it, and at that age I couldn't see myself having money in the future. I felt it was irresponsible to have a child without the money to raise it through college."* Miriam is a lesbian in a committed relationship, but she recalls a previous relationship with a woman she came close to changing her mind for. *"We were together for fifteen years, so at the age of thirty-nine I decided to try. It was an old story. You know, we weren't getting along well, so why not just have a child for some company? I agreed to undergo...what's it called?...insemination! See, I blocked it out. That's how much I didn't really want it! And deep down I knew it wouldn't work. My cycle had always been very erratic, and in my early relationships with men I had been careless, thinking that I was infertile. It was a stupid thing to think when I was young, but it turned out to be true. Now I am very, very happy, ecstatic even, that insemination didn't work. I was trying to save a relationship that was doomed. Even though I would have loved him or her, I would be really bummed now because the relationship was ending anyway and I would have ended up a single mother."*

If your preference is not to have children, then it is a safe bet that single motherhood is even less appealing. As we saw in the previous chapter, many women—whether married, coupled or single—cite the fear of becoming a single mother as a major deterrent to having children. It is not, however, because childfrees have jumped onto the single-mother-bashing bandwagon so prevalent in this patriarchy. Instead, it is the staggering awe at the tremendous responsibility of being a parent, let alone a single parent, that fosters caution. Many women feel that the risk of ending up alone with the kids is too great.

Danielle, thirty-nine, was raised by an extremely stressed single mom, so she knows firsthand what that job entails. *"I think there's a lot more at stake for women than just bearing the child and all of the physical responsibilities. There is also the risk of being a single mother, which would have a huge impact on a woman's life. Divorce and single motherhood are still stigmatized, and most of the time when there's divorce, the kids will end up with Mom. You could end up the only caregiver."*

Her husband of ten years, Joe, forty, agrees that in today's world the risk a woman takes is bigger than the risk for a man. *"If I came home tomorrow and said I really wanted to have kids, and she said no, then that would be the final word. It is definitely a different level of decision for a woman than it is for a man. We don't have to carry the child, give birth to the child, and that whole process. Plus, there is much more societal pressure on women around work, how they raise their children, and how they spend their time than on men.*

No matter how egalitarian we want to be, there is no way around the fact that women still carry the burden of childbearing to a much greater extent than men. Certainly the physical toll of childbearing accounts for a big part of that, but we all know that if a relationship fails, the job of full-time babysitter is most likely going to land with the mother. Here are some more fun facts about single motherhood that should be considered:

- One in two marriages ends in divorce, so if you have kids there is a good chance of being a single parent. (5)
- Single mothers make up 84 percent of single-parent households. While the single mothers far outnumber the single fathers, their status is as second-class citizens, while the rarely seen single father is admired. (6)
- Children of divorce (and thus their mothers) are five times more likely to live in poverty than children of intact families. (7)
- Only about 37 percent of single mothers receive regular child support. (8)
- In the year following a divorce, the standard of living for a man increases by an average of 10 percent, while the standard of living for a woman decreases by 27 percent. (9)
- The average child support received by single mothers is $1,331/year. (10) Deadbeat dads are rarely prosecuted. Even where strong enforcement laws exist, the adequate staff to back them up is lacking, proving the old adage that you can't get blood from a stone.

This picture is bleak and understandably strikes fear into the hearts of many women. While the fear of single parenthood should not be the sole factor in deciding whether or not to have kids, if you are considering compromising (acquiescing) for the sake of saving a relationship, think again! Chances are, you will only prolong the inevitable demise of the partnership, and when it does finally fail, you will be on your own with a child you didn't really want—forever!

NOT-SO-EVIL STEPMOTHERS

For single childfrees out there looking for love, there is one final parenting question to consider: stepparenting. Some of us, like Paula, thirty-nine, are very clear that it's not an option. "*I have no interest in dating anyone or becoming involved with anyone who wants kids or who has kids. I definitely don't want to be a stepparent.*" That is clear. For others, there are some shades of gray. Stacey, thirty-eight, has been married for five years to a childfree man, but said about her single days, "*I would've considered being a stepparent, but that wasn't my first choice. I didn't want all of that baggage. On the other hand, I had stepparents myself, and they were wonderful people. So, certainly that can work out.*" For Kathy, fifty-one, it was also the baggage issue that made her hesitant. "*When I was dating, it was definitely my preference to date people who did not have children. What I realized is that if the man has children, then the ex-wife is always going to be part of your life. There is never a clean break, and I really didn't want to deal with that.*"

Dating people who already have children means opening yourself up to the distinct possibility of being a sort-of parent, as well as a number of other potential pitfalls. Here are some questions to consider well in advance:

- Is stepparenting even something you are open to? If not, do not date people with kids, period.
- What are the ages of the children in question? If they are grown or a year or two from leaving the

nest, it may be more appealing than if they are very young.
- What is the parents' custody agreement? Are we talking 50/50 here, or just an occasional weekend?
- What is the potential partner's relationship with the ex? Once you start parenting someone else's children, territorial issues can easily arise.

Allison is a twenty-four-year-old woman engaged to a man with two kids, ages six and ten. *"I had reservations about the fact that he had kids. When I met him over two years ago, it was very clear that they came as a package deal. I had to be very sure that I could handle it before I really committed to him. There was a lot of thinking on my part. I always knew I didn't want my own children, so I had to decide if I wanted to be in that role, especially being as young as I am. The first part of our relationship was long distance, so when I decided to commit to Mike permanently I still hadn't met the kids. I moved cross-country and we moved in together right away. We have the kids fifty percent of the time, and the hardest thing about the adjustment was the loss of privacy. I really like and was used to having time alone in my house. Kids want your attention at all times and that was really difficult for me. I would lock myself in the bedroom and read or do something to try to get that space. It's still a process that we're working through. We're not one hundred percent comfortable as a family yet, but it did help that the kids were immediately very open to me, and I was doing my very best to be open to them."* As the adjustment period settled down, Allison began to notice some ways her life had changed. *"It's strange, but as a soon-to-be stepmother, I have partial access to a world I never had before. People with kids want to talk to me about my stepkids, and they think they can relate to me now, but I'm really stuck between two worlds. On the one hand, I have kids around to talk about with parents, but on the other hand, people without kids don't feel like they identify with me anymore because I'm no longer completely childfree. It's interesting having friends who have kids and friends who don't. You can't really talk about the same things with either group, because parents always want to talk about kids and the childfree have no interest in hearing anything about that at all. So I'm only able to talk about one part of my life with one set of people, and another part of my life with another set of people, and they're mutually exclusive."*

Hopefully, over time Alison will be as happy with her decision to stepparent as Kathleen, fifty-three, is. *"I have two stepchildren who are twenty and eighteen, but were six and four when I came together with their father. The younger one doesn't even remember a time without me. He's always had a 'Kate.' Because I grew up hearing repeatedly 'when you grow up, get married, and have children,' I always thought that I would have kids. Still, I was kind of an anomaly in my family because I didn't get married right out of high school, I went to college. After that I moved far away from home, which was also unusual for us. When I was forty or so I met my husband, who already had two little kids. When we first started talking about getting married, he told me that if I really wanted to have a child he would consider it, but he felt complete with two kids already. Then came our first weekend together with his children. He was out doing the yard and all that guy stuff while I was inside doing kid stuff, and I remember being completely exhausted. I kept looking at my watch and thinking,* Isn't it time for them to go home now? *It finally hit me that I didn't have it in me, so I told my husband thanks, but no thanks. I soon realized that I wanted to parent but not necessarily be a mother, and here was this wonderful man in my life with two little ones.*

I am blessed with a wonderful relationship with my stepkids, who are now just about grown, but when they were little and I got to do all that mommy stuff—like drive to school and make snacks and read stories until Daddy came home—it was magical. I got to parent without being a parent, and I feel like I had the best of that. Because I was always raised with the idea that you grow up, get married, and have kids, I always said to my stepkids, 'When you grow up, if you choose to get married or be partnered and you choose to have children, puppies or kittens, or whatever,' so that they always felt they had a choice. One day when my stepdaughter was a teenager she turned to me and said, 'Okay, Kate, we get it. We are going to choose our future and you didn't get to.' It made me laugh, but I wanted them to know that they may or may not have marriage and children, and either way it is okay."

Hopefully, someday soon more kids will be taught that marriage and babies are a choice, but for now the old refrain is alive and well: "When you grow up, get married, and have children...when you grow up, get married, and have children...when you grow up, get married, and have children." This familiar affirmation that many of us heard repeatedly during our youth is full of assumptions about what adult life will be. The childfree have already chucked the "have children" part from this three-part equation, but for the singletons out there, you're chucking two (if you consider yourself grown up, that is!). The assumption that coupled is better than single is akin to the assumption that child-burdened is better than childfree. But it's not necessarily so, according to some happy singletons who are bucking not just the baby train, but the relationship train as well. Being single by choice has about as much cachet as being childless by choice, largely due to the above mantra being repeated ad nauseam. But again, as with having kids, we find the notion that coupled is better than single is lacking any support from the data or research.

HAPPILY EVER AFTER – SINGLE

This "fairy tale" made its way into my email from an unknown source.

Once upon a time, a guy asked a girl, "Will you marry me?" The girl said, "NO!" And the girl lived happily ever after. She went shopping, dancing, camping, drank martinis, always had a clean house, never had to cook, did whatever the hell she wanted, never argued, traveled more, had many lovers, didn't save money, and had all the hot water to herself. She went to the theatre, never watched sports, never wore friggin' lacy lingerie that went up her ass, had high self-esteem, never cried or yelled, felt and looked fabulous in sweatpants, and was pleasant all the time. The End.

Like this story, Bella DePaulo, Ph.D. debunks the "married is better" myth in her book, *Singled Out: How Singles Are Stereotyped, Stigmatized, and Ignored, and Still Live Happily Ever After.* Much like the falsehood that children bring happiness, which is not supported by the research (see chapter 1), the marriage myth perpetuates the notion that our elusive bliss lies waiting in a union sanctioned by the church and/or state. While studies have been done that clearly show married participants as happier than unmarried participants, the inference that marriage must then lead to happiness is faulty science. DePaulo calls these studies "one-time happiness studies" (11), because they take a snapshot of one point in time and then draw conclusions about the joys of coupledom based on that. However, these studies make no attempt to analyze how happy these people were to begin with, what effect divorce or widowhood would have on the snapshot, or whether the happy married people stayed happy over time. In fact, one long-term happiness study done in Germany showed very little difference in overall happiness for marrieds versus singles, and another study showed adult happiness in countries with lower divorce rates to be less in married people than in singles. Using some of the speculation techniques so popular in these studies, I have inferred that it is the pressure to stay in a bad marriage that accounts for the differences.

Regardless of the facts, the band plays on, singing the praises of the joy of marriage. Yet, in areas of the United States where more traditional family values are preached as the only path, we find the highest divorce rates. The Bible Belt, for all its finger-wagging, has the highest divorce rate in the country. For example, the divorce rate in Arkansas is 5.9/1,000; in Alabama it is 4.9/1,000; and in Tennessee it is 4.6/1,000. In contrast, more liberal Massachusetts has the lowest divorce rate, 2.2/1,000, and New York is also lower at 2.8/1,000. (12) One could conclude that perhaps moral pressure in more conservative states can coax one into marriage, but can't make a bad marriage good. It is possible that people in Massachusetts or New York engage in more cohabitation that doesn't show up in the statistics, yet coupledom in itself does not seem to be the redeemer of the unhappy or the granter of joy any more than parenthood is.

DePaulo also portrays the coupled similarly to the way childfrees often describe parents: "Many people who practice marriage and coupling have sensed their special status and gotten greedy. Couples expect their love to be the only love that matters, and their goals and values to be the standards against which all other lives are measured. I don't see why we can't value coupling in a mature way, as one possible component of a life worth living rather than as a mandatory requirement imposed on all." (13) Much like the decision to live childfree, the decision to lead the single life has many secret joys and rewards. So if staying single or being happily single for now is your thing—carry on!

Cindy A. is a forty-three-year-old entrepreneur who is happily single and childfree, but in her early adulthood she was still under the assumption that you grow up, get married, and have children. *"I met someone and got married, because that was just what you did. It wasn't long after that I found myself mother, caregiver, and babysitter for an adult adolescent. When people asked us about kids, I said we weren't sure. As time went on, I began to realize that I did not want to have children with this man, and for the first time I asked myself the deeper question: did I want to have children with **any** man? I started reading books like* The Mommy Myth, *I spent time with a counselor, and I even consulted a psychic. I realized that the only reason I envisioned children in my life was because I had never been told there was an alternative. When my marriage ended, I realized that I could do anything. I left my job, started my own business, moved halfway across the country, and began dating. I really love the life I have made for myself. I love being single and I love being childfree. I think when I say that, people don't believe me, especially family. They think I* *put on a smile to cover up my true feelings of loss and loneliness. It is not true, but sometimes I find it easier to just let them believe that than try to convince them otherwise."*

Convincing others that we are happy without a partner or kids can be daunting, because the myth that marriage and children create happiness is so deeply ingrained in our psyches. It starts with the childhood taunt about "(Girl) and (boy) sitting in a tree, K-I-S-S-I-N-G, first comes love, then comes marriage, then comes (girl) with a baby carriage." People like Cindy A. know better and don't feel the need to convince others of their contentment; it is enough to have it.

THE CASE OF THE DISAPPEARING PEERS

With the scarcity of popular role models, many childfrees look to each other for support. All too often as we move toward our thirties and forties, those we once counted as friends begin to have children, changing those relationships forever. No matter how much we try or how tolerant we are of children, something is irrevocably changed.

"It has happened to me so many times," says Nicole, thirty-eight. *"New moms want to hang out with other people who have kids, and I don't blame them. They have something in common and they want to be together. Recently I made this new friend, and she's really great. I enjoy being with her, but I know she's going to want to start having babies soon. So I wonder how much I should really put into this new relationship. I know that sounds selfish, but I know from experience that as soon as she has babies I will hardly see her."*

Ellie, thirty-eight, has also had to say good-bye to friends once they had children. As happened with Nicole, the experience made her a bit cautious when developing new friends. *"I had two close friendships that changed once they had kids. I actually was the one who backed off, though. I wasn't rude; I just wanted to go my own way. I didn't want to hear about the latest diaper story and play dates and birthday parties. I think they probably felt they weren't getting the same from me, either. They wanted to talk to someone who could relate, and my life was totally different from theirs. My husband and I have these new friends now who don't have kids and are in their mid-thirties. We had dinner with them and I asked if they were planning on having kids one day. They said they had just had that conversation and decided not to. I had a great feeling of relief because I knew we could remain friends."*

Danielle, thirty-nine, and Joe, forty, also have made adjustments when friends have kids. A horse lover who spends lots of time with her equestrian friends, Danielle understands why parents seem to gravitate to each other. *"The friendship most affected after a child was born was with the couple across the street. They went from being always available to do stuff at the last minute to pretty much unavailable. If we want to get together it's always something like ordering takeout, and everything is scheduled around the kid's time clock. They were going through life happy-go-lucky, and all of a sudden it's every night at home entertaining the kid. Because they don't want to watch too much TV, we see them through the window looking like trained seals, clapping and hollering. The thing is that people with kids often want to talk to other people with kids so they can share stories and swap ideas, and they never get sick of talking about it. I guess it's like the horse people for me. We talk about horses nonstop and we never get sick of hearing about it. But they're the only people that I could talk about that stuff with nonstop. So I do understand why they do that, because I have it, too, just with a different topic."*

Parents, horse lovers, and childfrees all need community. The amount of social support childfree adults find will depend largely on where they live, what their family is like, and whom they associate with. Those who live in a diverse urban community may find many childfree adults who at best support their choice, and at worst don't really care.

Janet, forty-four, and her husband are an urban couple who have no trouble finding like-minded adults to connect with. *"There's a whole community of people in the world who do not want to have kids, and I have built my life around those kinds of people. Every now and then I will meet a woman who doesn't want to have kids who says, 'Oh, I am so glad to meet someone like you; I don't know anyone like you.' It surprises me because my whole social circle is people like me. They're out there, but maybe that is a Portland thing."*

Conversely, childfrees who live in more traditional, conservative surroundings can easily find themselves alone, marginalized, or even ganged up on. These types of experiences can lead to self-doubt about what was formerly an ironclad, well-thought-out decision.

Page, forty-four, has been with her husband for twenty-five years. *"I had a six-month period where I was questioning myself. I kept thinking about how we were getting older and it was only the two of us. Plus, I was surrounded by childhood friends who all had families. At that time, I reached out to the No Kidding network for support, and it has been great. It put those thoughts aside because I had community again. It was so refreshing to be around people who were comfortable with their decision not to have kids. It was an about-face from the usual objections, and it put any doubts to rest."*

Being surrounded by nothing but parents is not only isolating, it can be downright annoying. Scott, forty-one and married, burns out on kid talk fairly quickly. *"One thing that annoys me is when you go places and people who are parents just can't seem to shut up about how great their kid is. It's all they know anymore and the only thing that they can talk about. Now we belong to this group, No Kidding, and it's a fantastic thing. There's a whole bunch of people our age who don't have kids and we can talk about things that don't involve kids. That's very nice."*

Before finding fellowship in No Kidding, Pam, thirty-nine, and her husband of twelve years were having trouble balancing time with the kids in their family and their own needs. *"Even though we really love spending time with our nieces and nephews, there's pressure to go to every birthday party, and every holiday revolves around what's convenient for the kids. They all live between one and three hours away, so it's not like they are around the corner. I struggled with how much should be expected of me and whether it makes me a bad aunt if we don't go to one birthday party. Before we found our local No Kidding chapter it was really getting to be a problem. We've thought,* Gee, we decided not to have children, but our lives completely revolve around them anyway. *Now we've met a lot of new people and are busy with them, and that really helps the situation a lot. If we don't want to go to a family gathering, we can genuinely say that we have plans and we can't go."*

Whether you already have a circle of childfree friends, are looking for your peers, or need some advice on balancing family pressures with your personal life, there are a couple of good resources you can try. Web site clearinghouse www.childfree.net hosts an ongoing conversation of childfree people around issues of all sorts, well beyond the kid stuff. Members of this Listserv act as sounding boards for each other and are a great resource for advice and opinions. If chatting online isn't your thing and you prefer social interaction, www.nokidding.net is for you. This group is a social network with chapters all over the world. Some chapters are very active and host lots of events, while others are a means for connecting with other childfrees in your area. You can find a group near you or, if there isn't one in your area, get help starting one. If you feel isolated, like you are the only one in the world who feels the way you do, you're not! The worst thing you could do for yourself, your partner, and most of all an unborn soul, is acquiesce in order to "fit in," only to find the pain and misery of your decision worse than what you are dealing with now.

Beyond the emotional cost of having an unwanted child, you must also consider the financial cost. Each year the Department of Agriculture publishes an estimate of the cost to raise one child in America today. The current estimate is $180,000–$270,000, depending on income, to rear a child to the age of eighteen. (14) However, this number covers only the basic care and feeding of a child. What happens to that number when you factor in things like extracurricular activities, college, lost wages for the caregiving parent, and/or day care? Phillip Longman factors in all of those things in his book *The Empty Cradle*, and comes up with a number much closer to a million dollars when all is said and done. (15) If you are feeling pressured by a partner, friends, or family, it is extremely important to ask yourself, *Do I have twenty-two years and a million dollars to spare on this experiment?* And that is the best-case scenario, which does not factor in the possibility of having a special needs child who requires care until the day you leave this earth and beyond.

The world of dating is sticky for anyone. As childfree adults, we have one more awkward hurdle to get past. But when you do, and you find that special someone who says, "Hey, I don't want kids, either!"—it is beautiful. A childfree union can provide new opportunities, adventures, and ever-deepening closeness. Married twenty-five years, Page describes their marvelous journey together like this: "*The first twelve years of our marriage are such a blur. We moved around the globe for his job, Hong Kong, Indonesia, Malaysia. Then we even lived a year apart while I finished graduate school in Maine and he was in Germany. We saw each other one week a month, which made it more bearable, but it would have been impossible with kids. It really cemented our relationship in a way that I never would have imagined. That is one thing people with kids may miss. One of my high school girlfriends said I'd never know love because I hadn't had kids, but her marriage will probably never get to the point mine has because they have kids. It really irks me that she would say I'd never know love. We are so reliant on each other and such good friends. We are so much more a unit even though we are independent. When we got married, the minister said the best part of marriage is twenty years down the road. I think what he meant was that once the hard part of raising a family is over, you will then really begin to appreciate this person you have spent so much time with. Well, we skipped that raising a family part and our relationship is so easy, fun, and entertaining. My husband travels a lot for work and we both are fine on our own, but we recently took a trip to France where we were together twenty-four hours a day for a week and we had a wonderful time.*"

You don't have to have children—or even a partner, for that matter—to make a family. Most of us have a few special people in our lives we consider family, even though we're not actually related. A wonderful tale of the families that are made when two childfrees find each other and fall in love is Laura Carroll's *Families of Two*. The book certainly helped Louise, thirty-nine, who said, *"I will make a lot of accommodations for friends who are new moms so that the friendship can survive. However, a friend of mine had a baby and started saying things like, 'People who have families...' or 'You don't have a family.' I said, 'Yes, I do. My husband and I are a family.' She said, 'Well, you know what I mean.' But I didn't know what she meant, because we are a family! In addition, I have a lot of things that parents don't have, like a deeper relationship with my husband. That's why I really loved Laura Carroll's book."*

While the revelation that you don't want children can bring a first, second, or tenth date to a screeching halt, the earlier that tidbit gets worked into the conversation, the better for everyone. It may seem risky or presumptuous, but the longer you wait the harder it will be should the other person not share your feelings. However, there is a light at the end of the tunnel, and if finding a childfree mate is the goal, then put it out there early in any new relationship. One of these times you will look across the table and hear those wonderful words, "Really? You don't want kids? Me, neither!" After that, who knows?

5

But I Want Grandchildren!

Relationships based on obligation lack dignity.... If you are living out of a sense of obligation, you are a slave.

—Wayne Dyer

Growing up in California suburbia, I was constantly surrounded by kids with the latest cool thing that I wasn't allowed to have: designer jeans, fancy cars, the newest music or stereo system. I felt envious and left out. Like most kids, I would go home and beg, plead, and relentlessly badger my parents in hopes that they would get me the latest and greatest doodad. "It's not fair!" I would shout. "All my friends have one!" To which my parents would simply respond (all together now), "Life isn't fair!"

So now the tables are turned. Your parents see something cool and exciting that all of *their* friends have. Something that makes them feel envious and left out. Now it is their turn to beg, plead, and badger you. "It isn't fair! All of my friends have grandchildren!" But the conventional wisdom they taught us so well remains tried and true. "Life isn't fair."

NO MEANS NO

Not only is life unfair, but sometimes it may even seem cruel. Many parents of childfree adults worked hard and raised their children with the dream of one day enjoying grandchildren. After all, most of our parents grew up in a time when there were no alternatives. Now they are seeing the whole plan halted by offspring who choose to remain childfree. Many older adults feel great pain when their kids don't go on to have kids of their own. Their plans for the future are shattered, and an expectation that has been consistent through countless generations is ending. However, I can't help questioning the motivation of parents who pressure their childfree children to procreate. Oftentimes, they even have grandchildren by other children, but still try to scare their childfree kid with claims like, "you'll never really be happy" or "it's different when they're your own," insisting that the decision to forgo parenting will only lead to unhappiness and despair. It seems like they are worried about their child's happiness, but really it is not about that. The real motivation is plain and simple—selfishness. It's probably not intentional or premeditated, and they may very well believe their concerns are about their adult child and not themselves. However, when what parents want for their child becomes more important than what the child wants for herself, what else can be said?

Childfree adults handle parental pressure in different ways. Some have parents who are understanding and don't apply baby pressure, regardless of whether there are siblings to provide them with grandchildren. Pam has a sister who recently had a baby, but well before that she still enjoyed her parents' support. *"My parents have been very accepting of my decision. My mother told me once that she admired the fact that I had really thought it through. Now that my sister has a baby, we are hearing about how much they wanted to be grandparents, but they never put that on us. Both my parents have supported our decision."* More and more childfrees are experiencing this kind of acceptance. As subsequent generations begin to make reproduction a choice and not an obligation, this acceptance should only increase.

Childfrees who are only children or have childfree/childless siblings may be on the hot seat to a greater degree than those with parenting siblings. Kathy, fifty-one, is an only child and has had to face telling her mother there will be no grandchildren. *"In the beginning, my mother was not happy about my decision not to have children, because I was her only chance. She always pictured herself retired and watching my child and all that. Now what she does is fawn over my friends when they have children. My assistant at work had a baby, and my mother loves to come and have lunch with us. She always asks her to bring the baby, and then she makes a big fuss over them both, not to mention any other little babies around. Sometimes I feel like that's a subtle insult to me. Here her daughter has this great education, wonderful job with great money, is really independent and all of that, but if only she had a baby, then she would be complete. My mother has always been very needy and built her whole life around me. I don't know if it's something that she's missing in her life or if she wishes that she had other children or what. I just wish it wasn't so important to her. Eventually, she did come to terms with the fact that I'm not going to have any children and doesn't say anything directly to me anymore. Instead, she says it with her actions."*

Danielle, thirty-nine, is also an only child, and unfortunately her mother still has not come to terms with not being a grandma. *"My mom thinks that I am completely wrong, and that there's something seriously wrong with me. Why would I not want to have kids? Why would I deny my husband, Joe? Why would I deny her? What's my problem? She thinks that it's her right to have grandchildren. I have tried to help her understand that it's a decision I've made that's in my best interests, and it's really none of her business. Regardless, we still go through it every couple of years"*

Then some of us have scores of nieces and nephews and still suffer the scorn of parents who feel let down. Natalie has plenty of nieces and nephews, but is still under pressure. *"My dad is not happy about our decision not to have kids, and he doesn't even really want to talk to me about it. If it comes up, he always says, 'You know how I feel about that.' He's disappointed, which doesn't make sense to me because he has lots of grandchildren. My sister has four kids and my brother has three. I think he secretly thinks that we're going to change our minds, but that's not going to happen. For whatever reason, he's one of those people who believe that you should have kids. It's just something you should do."*

Navigating the minefield of parental objections is a tricky business. Childfrees all handle it differently, depending on their personalities, their "tension tolerance thresholds," and the nature of their parental relationships. Some childfree adults are very open about their status and let the chips fall where they may.

Kristen started to hear clamoring for grandchildren as soon as she and Scott got married. *"For the longest time, my parents would ask me and ask me about us having kids. Finally I had to tell them to stop. I said, 'I don't want children. Please stop; leave me alone; it's none of your business. There is nothing you can say to change my mind. It's a personal decision, so leave me alone.' After many years, my mother finally came around and said she was fine with it. I said, 'Great, but even if you aren't, it's my life, and it's my decision.'"*

Kristen stuck to her guns, and when her sister had a child things did change. *"My sister had a baby and my mother finally got to be a grandma. Now she says things like, 'It's so nice to be with you because I can actually talk to you without being interrupted. When you spend time with me you are with me.' Of course, when she's with my sister, she's running around with the kids and always distracted."*

Lisa is an outspoken nursing student in Portland, Oregon, but her roots are small town. *"I come from a very small town in rural Ontario where you're expected to have children. When I was in high school, there were a lot of girls getting pregnant, and then they would bring their children to school. My mother always thought I'd be the one to provide the granddaughter, since my brother has boys, but I told her no. I have always been very open about my childfree status and that really made me stand out. I wanted to stand out and be different, which is very hard to do in a small town. So I wore my childfree status like a badge of honor."*

Jennifer M., thirty-six, told her parents at a very young age, but they didn't buy it at first. *"I told my parents when I was twelve that I didn't want children, but of course they thought I would change my mind. When I got older, I was told that I was evil, unnatural, and selfish. Who would take care of me when I got old? Who would marry me? Then there was the sobbing over how there would be no grandchildren. Next, they started taking over my cousins' kids and treating them like grandchildren. It got worse, but I have blocked most of their ridiculous accusations out of my head and can't remember them all."*

Given the potential for major family conflict, other childfree adults may choose to be more private about their decisions, allowing friends and/or family to believe that "it just didn't happen." While no one wants to live a lie, for some childfrees the pressure is so disruptive to life and family, the "don't ask, don't tell" policy is their best solution. Playing both sides of the fence has been the path of least resistance for Jennifer H., twenty-nine, a very ambitious law student who is working to pass the bar exam and manage a household with her husband of six years. *"I had my tubes tied at twenty-three years old, before we got married. That is one thing that our parents don't know. We told them when we got married that we didn't want kids, but we didn't tell them about my tubal. It has been easier to let them hold out a little bit of hope than crush them with the news. Now that I am a bit older and they are more accepting, I wouldn't want to reveal that I had been keeping it from them, or lie and say I just did it, so we aren't going to say anything. Fact is, it is really none of their business."*

As in the case of an overstressed parent trying to control a toddler's tantrum, the temptation to simply "give in" and let pleading parents have their way can be intense. Most childfrees really love their parents and feel sorry to disappoint them. It is perfectly normal for childfree adults in this situation to feel guilty or remorseful. But rumor has it that a child is a lifelong commitment that, unlike designer jeans, a new stereo, or even an adorable puppy, cannot be returned or cast aside after a brief thrill ride. Just because someone else does something, that doesn't mean you should do it, right? That's a lesson I learned in childhood from Mom and Dad when they lectured, "If Susie jumped off a bridge, would you jump off a bridge?"

I recommend being open about the decision to be childfree and discussing it with your parents. If they are not open to it, speak to a counselor or reach out to the childfree community discussed in the previous chapter and get some support. If your parents are having a difficult time with your decision, at least be sure you are not. The more comfortable you feel with your decision, the more likely they are to accept it. It is a far smaller offense to disappoint a parent than to bring another unwanted child into this overcrowded world.

BE CAREFUL WHAT YOU WISH FOR

Many grandparents have discovered, much to their chagrin, what can happen when their children thoughtlessly procreate. The number of grandparents who have become burdened with raising a grandchild or grandchildren late in life because their kids didn't or couldn't do it is on the rise. The issues faced in raising grandchildren are far more complicated than in raising one's own children. Emotional problems, legal issues, and financial burdens can ravage a well-deserved retirement.

According to the U.S. Census Bureau, in 2000:

- There were 3.9 million children living with grandparents who were their sole caregivers, a 19 percent increase over the previous decade. (1)
- There were 2.4 million grandparents who reported being solely responsible for the care of grandchildren living with them. (2)

- Of these "grandfamilies," 19 percent live at or below the government's defined poverty line. (3)
- Untold numbers of "grandfamilies" live barely above the poverty line, making them less likely to receive benefits and/or public assistance. (4)

Our parents can be proud that we have not left them with that type of burden. However, when weighing the decision to have or not to have children, it is *your* wants and desires that matter most. It is far too big of a commitment and too important a responsibility to take on out of sheer obligation.

THE MISSING LINK

For some parents of the childfree, it is hard to understand their kids not wanting kids because their own drive to procreate was so strong. On the other hand, those who had very little interest in parenting themselves but lived in a time with few alternatives may be subconsciously compensating for the guilt they feel. Today, childfrees can discuss their lack of parental drive and its possible origins, nature or nurture, more openly. Michael, sixty-one, speculates, *"I would probably be the same kind of father I had, absentee. My half sister grew up with him, and she is also childfree. It shows that there is something to it in the genes. Whatever was missing in his genetics that made him an incompetent parent, I was lucky to catch in time."*

The nature versus nurture debate has yet to be unequivocally resolved on issues such as addiction or homosexuality, and now we can add the childfree to the list. Perhaps, like most things in life, it's a little of both.

Childfrees often hear that anyone who had a lousy childhood and doesn't want kids is simply running away from something. Parents of the childfree can be filled with worry that perhaps something they did during their child's early life is to blame. However, there are lots of people who had bad childhoods—even atrocious ones—and are now parents, just like there are many people who had blissful, idyllic childhoods who have chosen to remain childfree. Interestingly, all the childfree people I talked to—regardless of whether their childhoods were good or bad, and whether they always knew they didn't want children or came to that decision later in life—described a curious absence of maternal and/or paternal drive. Like a missing gene, the need to breed eludes them.

Although it is often assumed that the majority of childless women would prefer to be mothers, this is untrue. Current data indicates that for the last two decades the number of voluntarily childless women outnumbered the involuntarily childless by significant margins. From 1982 to 1995 the number of voluntarily childless women between the ages of thirty-five and forty-four went from 5 percent to 9 percent and then ebbed down to 7 percent in 2002. However, during that same time period, the number of involuntarily childless women remained a constant 4 percent. (5) As with infertility, it is possible that the lack of desire to parent has a physiological component—inherited from the parents through genetics. While a desirous grandparent may not like to hear this, if he or she is at all to blame for the absence of grandchildren, it is possibly due to heredity as much as or more than upbringing. More research is needed in this area to know for sure.

Nicole is a thirty-eight-year-old business owner. *I've known I didn't want kids since I was in high school. That seems pretty young to know such a thing, but I've never been drawn to the parenting lifestyle. I'm not a baby person. I think it's a gene missing or something. You know how sometimes you see those women going crazy over babies? I am just not like that. Bring me a puppy and I'm all over it, but not a baby."*

Many of the people I interviewed pondered the nature-versus-nurture question when it comes to being childfree, often reporting that they believe one or both of their parents would have been childfree if given the chance. Vicki, forty-six, commented, *"My father continues to praise me for my decision. He says, 'Don't get me wrong; I love all the kids and grandkids, but you made the wisest decision by not having any.' I think he would've opted not to have children if he could've. He was a good father, but he was very detached. He was not interested in hanging out with us, and I knew from a very early age that he was a provider more than one to goof around with."*

Vicki is not alone in her suspicions. Lee, a fifty-one-year-old nutritional therapist, was one of three daughters. *"I think that if my mother had had her druthers she certainly wouldn't have had three children. Maybe she wouldn't have had any, but there wasn't an option for her. I was born in 1956, when suburbia was really starting to boom. Even though she had three children, my mother made it very clear that she would not move into a suburban home or become a Stepford wife. The same is true of my mother-in-law, who said to me one time, 'I don't know if I would have had kids, given a choice.' That really surprised me because she idolized my husband. He was her firstborn and the center of her life. But when I thought about it, I realized both our mothers were of a generation where it really wasn't a choice."*

Some of us can trace our childfree origins not only to a parent, but also to very early childhood memories. For instance, Lori, the forty-three-year-old paralegal, was six years old when she announced her intention to be childfree. *"There was a day I will never forget. A neighbor*

was pregnant and we had just been to her house. I was play-
ing in the front yard and I had dolls with me, and I started
thinking about having kids. I literally dropped my dolls right
there because it made me physically sick. Panicked, I went to my
mother and said, 'I don't want to have babies!' It was such a
visceral reaction and it has been that way ever since."

Then there's Eileen, a forty-eight-year-old journeyman printer who declared at age five that she didn't
want kids. *"In the childfree community, that is what we call*
an early articulator," she says. But not all are blessed with
such clarity so early.

Pam is thirty-nine and happily childfree. However,
growing up she always thought she wanted to have children. *"I guess I always assumed that I would. It didn't occur to*
me not to, because that's just what you do. When I got married,
my husband was still in college and we didn't even talk about
it. It wasn't until later that I realized I didn't want children. It
didn't appeal to me." The lack of desire to be a parent is a
common theme among the consciously childfree.

The mystery remains, though, why anyone would try
to talk someone who didn't want children into having
them. Is it a real belief that their children need children
to be happy? Is it the selfish desire to be a grandparent
disguised as well-meaning guidance? Is it suppressed
regret over having children themselves? In the absence
of any real data on their motives, one can only speculate.
However, when we make the choice to have children
just that—a choice—the likelihood of regret decreases.
It is far better that people who don't want children be
supported in their decision than harassed into joining
the parenting team. The parents of the childfree hopefully will realize that their adult children have lots to
contribute to our world in other forms, as do they.

FILL YOUR OWN BUCKET

Parents of the childfree have lots of love to give. They want to shower a grandchild with all the fun, free-wheeling attention they had to temper as their child's disciplinarian. Chances are they do not, however, want to become the disciplinarian or sole provider again. If influencing the next generation is something they feel strongly about, there are other ways to bring children into their lives. Lots of kids out there could use their love and devotion. Becoming a foster grandparent, volunteering at a school, or working in a shelter are some ways grandchild-less adults can get involved. There are so many ways to channel that grandparent love for the benefit of all society.

Those of us who have parents who really enjoyed the job may find them hard to convince. They persist with, "You won't ever be happy unless you have children." From their perspective, this probably feels very true. After all, *they* couldn't have been happy without children. Building a family gave their lives meaning and purpose. They loved the job and can't imagine anyone not wanting it. Of course, just because something made one person happy doesn't mean it would make everyone happy. The world has become far too complex for a one-size-fits-all formulaic existence. Whether we are single, coupled, married, gay, or straight, we all have our own personal wants, desires, and purpose. For some, that still means "grow up, get married, and have children," but for an increasing number of us, that means remaining childfree.

6
Who Will Take Care of You When You're Old?

We are made wise not by the recollection of our past, but by the responsibility for our future.

—George Bernard Shaw

We see them in the streets, shuffling across an intersection, frantically trying to make it across before the light turns green. Dressed in ratty clothing, dragging a rusted cart full of scraps, these elderly throwaways could be you or me. How did this happen? Where are their families? Did they have any children? What if that happens to me? In the age of the ever-shrinking nuclear family, the fear of ending up old and alone looms large.

With the recent economic meltdown, these fears are increasing among all Americans, childfree or not. Pension plans are going bankrupt, retirement accounts have been raided by unscrupulous Wall Street investors, and the plummeting stock market has devastated 401k plans for countless workers. Social Security and Medicare are vilified as wasteful, unnecessary taxes, even though analysis has shown that without them almost half of all seniors would have incomes at or below the poverty line. (1) Back in 1935, when Social Security was implemented, average life expectancy was 61.7 years, but today that number is up to 77.6 years. (2) That seems like it should be good news, but unfortunately, the longer we live, the greater the likelihood that we will need assistance, and in a nation with deteriorating safety nets, that is a pretty scary proposition.

So, better get your insurance policy now. A couple of kids will surely guarantee safety and security as the years pass, right? Wrong. Today, very few adults are depending on children to care for them in old age, which is good, since very few adults are planning on taking care of their aging parents, either. Instead, many aging adults with children fear being a burden to them in later years. Research conducted for AARP found that fewer than one-third of subjects aged forty-five and above report that they are depending on children or other family to care for them in old age. (3) Whom are they depending on, then? Interestingly, 68 percent said they would be able to depend on friends and family for small tasks that would allow them to stay in their homes as they age. (4) The conflict between how people answered the more general questions versus the more specific questions indicates that their assumptions and their realities may be skewed. As the study concluded: "There also appears to be some disconnect between what people say and what they do, or anticipate doing. For example, almost all respondents say it is likely that they will be able to stay in their current home for the rest of their life, but only about half anticipate they will need to make changes to their home as they age. Another example is that the majority of respondents say they are 'planners,' however fewer have given a great deal of thought to the home features or community characteristics they will need in their later years." (5)

NOT JUST A RIVER IN EGYPT

The reality derived from this is that, regardless of family status, there's a whole hill of denial going on when it comes to aging. In a society that worships youth and shuts its elderly away where no one has to see the inevitable ravages of time, it is really not surprising. However, whether one has children or not, failure to plan realistically for old age is a national problem with no easy solutions.

Lee, fifty-one and married, saw what happened to her in-laws when a split-second accident devastated their retirement. *"My husband's mother fell down the stairs a few years back and sustained a brain injury, much like having a stroke. After spending a summer in intensive care she went home, where her husband could not take care of her full time. They're both in their sixties, and they had to sell everything to pay for care. They had to basically go into poverty and file for bankruptcy in order to qualify for government help. Now, in order to get the care she needs, they can't make any money or have any income. They can't do anything or their help is cut off. It is completely asinine. It's quite a reminder for me about what you must lose in order to get any kind of help from the state. My husband and I both have good retirement funds, but when you look at how much things cost, I realize that if I had a stroke or something those funds could get wiped out pretty easily."*

With some exceptions, the majority of childfree people I interviewed were like the rest of America, preparing for retirement but totally unprepared for old age. I can't stress this enough: retirement and old age are two completely different things. End of life issues are the nine-hundred-pound gorilla in the room that no one wants to mention. Usually, we don't get around to dealing with end-of-life issues until someone we love is facing them. That someone may even be us. If you get to that spot without a plan, your options may be very limited. Yet this problem is not facing only the childfree. Adult children of the elderly often find themselves too bogged down with work and family stress of their own, not to mention geographical unavailability, to be relied on as caregivers.

Holly, forty-five, deflates the "who will take care of you when you're old" reaction to being childfree in one blow. *"When someone asks me who's going to take care of me when I get old, I ask them who's taking care of their parents. Ninety percent of the time it's not them, so that pretty much ends it right there. I feel like financially, my husband and I will be much better off than those who have children and spent all their money on things like clothing, braces, education, and whatnot. The reality is there are no guarantees that your kids will even like you, or that they will outlive you, or that they'll be in any kind of position to do anything for you."*

Janet, forty-four, knows kids are not an insurance policy. *"I have lots of aunts and uncles, all of whom have children, and their kids are either stealing from them or not doing squat for them. Some kids are not emotionally or financially equipped to take care of their elderly, sick parent. It is a lot more taxing than taking care of a child. I look at my dad, who is having a great retirement. He's eighty-four and still healthy. That's a good motivator for me to stay really healthy now. Basically, it's save money, stay healthy, and keep the stress down because it is so bad for you. Work, save money, but don't lose sight of balance."*

Even the best-laid plans, however, are no guarantee. There is an assumption I found prevalent among my interviewees that money is the answer. There's no doubt that it will be an essential factor. After all, we will need to pay out of pocket for whatever care we need beyond any residual Medicare. This is true for parents and non-parents alike. But to get that care there must be services available for purchase with our stash of cash. With the baby boomer generation quickly closing in on retirement, concerns about supply of services given the assured onslaught in demand has many senior advocates rightfully worried.

GETTING CARE THAT ISN'T THERE

In 2005, Washington D.C. held the fifth White House Conference on Aging (WHCoA), attended by leaders from the private and public sectors who serve our seniors and have their collective finger right on the pulse of things to come. Started in 1961, WHCoA is held once a decade to advise the president and Congress on policy issues facing the elderly and support the ongoing care and dignity of our seniors. Needless to say, there is much cause for concern, no matter what your reproductive choice.

It won't come as a shock to most that then-President George W. Bush decided to skip the once-a-decade conference, making him the first president not to address his own conference in the almost fifty years of its existence. To add insult to injury, while 1,200 delegates from around the country were meeting in an uptown hotel, Bush headed the opposite direction, to Greenspring Village, an upscale, gated retirement community located in Virginia, touting the glories of his Medicare drug benefit package slated to commence a few months later. While some praised the plan early on, reports are now confirming what many already knew—this program was nothing more than a boon to drug companies and private insurers. In fact, an analysis by the Congressional Oversight Committee revealed, "Since the Part D program went into effect in January 2006, the average list price for the 25 most popular drugs used by Part D beneficiaries has increased by 8.9%, almost twice as fast as the overall inflation rate." (6) If that weren't bad enough, additional findings showed that privatizing the Part D portion of Medicare resulted in administrative costs that are six times higher than those of traditional Medicare programs. All in all, the report found that "taxpayers and Medicare Part D beneficiaries could have saved almost $15 billion in 2007 if administrative expenses in the program were reduced to the level achieved by traditional Medicare and drug prices were lowered to Medicaid levels." (7)

Meanwhile, back at the WHCoA, an alarm bell was blaring the warning of serious shortfalls in senior services. Most alarming to the childfree will be the severe lack of caregivers, both family and professional.

Ellie is a thirty-eight-year-old married woman who was grilled by a co-worker as to who would care for her when she gets old. Her response was witty and wise: *"All the money that you are sinking into your kids and their education, my husband and I will put away, so that one day we will have caviar fed to us off golden spoons at the fanciest raisin farm you can find. It will be beautiful."*

There's just one flaw in that beautiful plan. According to a 2006 report, there may not be enough raisin farms to go around, and even if there are, staffing them with well-trained caregivers may be a problem. (8) As you read this, fifteen million Americans are using some sort of caregiving services, either at home or in specialized facilities. As exorbitant as that number seems, it's projected to be closer to thirty million by the year 2050. (9) For those of us between the ages of about twenty-five and fifty, this is the time in the future when we will be likely to need such services and the number most relevant to our futures. According to the analysis, 20 percent of older adults needing care right now can't find the help they need. (10) It is frightening to think of what that number will look like forty plus years into the future.

It is almost enough to scare us into having a child, if only for insurance. But before you do, consider that only 42 percent of seniors who receive in-home care get it from adult children, and even then there are costs. (11) Lost wages, benefits, and even jobs can put a severe burden on the adult child caregiver, demonstrating how having an adult child no more negates the need for financial resources than being childfree. Many family caregivers report strained relationships with spouses, loss of personal time and, perhaps worst of all, lost time with their own children. And the caregiver isn't the only one taking a hit. U.S. employers lose an estimated 33.6 billion dollars annually when family caregiving causes their workers to lose time and productivity. (12)

I have heard many adults point out how other cultures with extended families engaging in more traditional roles don't seem to have this problem. "In China, families take care of their aged parents," is an all-too-common refrain. However, China is one of the many countries with an extremely low birthrate compared to its aging population, and as China heads full-bore into industrialization, the problem of caring for the aged is emerging. Many young Chinese are finding themselves conflicted among the old ways, the new ways, and an even greater lack of elder-care options than we have. Add to that the lack of siblings to share the load, and a looming crisis may be on their horizon. In nations where parents working outside the home is the norm, caregiving for elders is a financial issue, whether one pays for caregiving or loses one's own potential wages to do it "for free." The trend toward this model is unlikely to change anytime soon, whether it is in the U.S. or emerging nations such as China.

Unlike most other modern nations, the United States operates in a free-market healthcare system, at least for the moment, that has resulted in a mishmash of services unequally distributed throughout the land, often leaving seniors and/or their family members bewildered, beleaguered, and underserved.

Without a standard of care in this country, we have to hope that some individual or entity will be around and available for hire at a rate we can afford. In chapter 3, we looked at the upcoming labor shortage in our graying nation. Finding qualified nurse's aides to work in what is a very difficult and poorly compensated job is already a challenge, and for good reason. Caregiving is one of the lowest-paid occupations in America, which speaks volumes about the value, or lack of value, we place on our seniors. At an average hourly rate of ten dollars for nurse's aides, less than nine dollars for in-home health aides, and eight dollars for personal care aides, there is hardly a line out the door of willing, let alone qualified, applicants. (13) Also, before you begin calculating the cost of a home health aide for yourself based on those numbers, keep in mind that they usually come from an agency that charges the client twice or more what it pays the aide. That means a ten-dollar-per-hour aide will cost the consumer twenty dollars per hour (14), thanks to our for-profit healthcare system. Projections indicate that the need for home healthcare workers is expected to increase by 56 percent over the next decade (15), which begs the question: where will they come from?

There are so many unanswered questions around aging in our society, it is no wonder we have put our heads in the sand. Tackling the graying of America and what that means for us as a nation only seems to enter the debate when Social Security and Medicare are concerned. End-of-life issues do not make for sexy campaign slogans or political platforms, so we will most likely be in full-bore crisis mode before acting. No one is looking out for our future but us, so the need to plan beyond retirement is crucial. Unfortunately, many of us are not even really planning for retirement, with the level of saving in America at an all-time low and the level of personal debt at an all-time high. Yet, while many of us do at least think about retirement planning, very few of us plan for old age. I said it before, but it bears repeating: retirement planning and old-age planning are not the same thing. Retirement is when one stops working a job and starts enjoying the "golden years" with travel, art, and other life pursuits that were put on hold while one was part of the workforce. Old age is when we are no longer able to do those things we think of as retirement because our bodies and/or minds are deteriorating. This is a natural part of the life cycle that as a society we don't want to look at.

So, how can we plan for old age when we know almost nothing about it? Just like people sometimes have kids, only to find that the realities of parenthood are not what they imagined, people know little of the realities of aging until they hit home. In both cases, our isolationist culture gets the blame. The nuclear-family social model provides little or no exposure to these major life transitions until they are upon us. Today, an entire generation is getting educated on the realities of having children and aging parents all at once.

SANDWICH GENERATION

The baby boomers, now being dubbed the "Sandwich Generation," are juggling the needs of school-age children with the difficulties of aging parents. Throw in the demands of their careers, marriages, or other life pursuits, and these folks are quickly getting a lot of reality. The number of middle-aged people with living elderly parents is bigger than ever before and will continue to increase over the next few decades. As women delay childbearing into their thirties and forties, the likelihood of having school-age children and ailing parents at the same time increases. Many adult children truly want to care for their ailing parents but are physically, emotionally, financially, or geographically unable.

Between working full time and raising their own children, there's not much left for aging parents.

Many children grew up with the belief that their parents would be self-sufficient in old age. They had spoken or unspoken assurances of their parents' intention not to burden the kids. Intentions are not guarantees, though, and when what was expected is not what comes, the results can be guilt, stress, and fear. No one planned for that, either.

Then there are those adult children who not only don't want to (or are unable to) care for their aging parents, but who resent their parents for spending their own money on care. After college I had the privilege of working in an elder-care facility that was chock-full of people who had children. Some were close to them and others were not, but there was one thing the vast majority of them had in common: they were paying their own way. What they got for their money was the care their family wasn't even asked to provide, but that didn't stop several residents' offspring from whining about the dwindling inheritance they would never see. Not pretty.

Adult children are not only unreliable for support in old age, but they can even turn the tables, becoming a financial liability when they are having struggles of their own. Many young adults are feeling the squeeze of the shrinking middle class and disappearing safety nets. As income goes down and the cost of living goes up, grown kids are more likely to need help than to provide help. During the last few decades, we have heard about the increasing move back to the nest and what that means for parents trying to reclaim their independence or enjoy retirement. Whether we call it "extended adolescence" or "adultescence," kids are taking longer to become self-sufficient than ever before. Many of my friends who have had babies in their forties joke about being almost sixty before they are "done," but sixty-five to seventy is more like it. With the huge debt being racked up by college students and a shrinking job market, it is no wonder that a 2009 survey by Monster.com revealed that two-thirds of grads are opting to move back home after college.

Low entry-level wages, high rents and housing prices, coupled with soaring tuition costs and the burden of school and other debts mean that children cannot afford to live the lifestyle their parents raised them in. Sometimes referred to as the "Boomerang Generation," kids today are more likely to remain a liability for longer. While some parents may be glad to help out their Boomerang kids, the fact is, this places a greater financial burden on them right at the time they really need to be socking it away for their own old age.

There seems to be no clear winner when it comes to aging. Parents and non-parents have their own sets of challenges to confront with the passing of time. The point is that having children to stave off some fear of old age is an incredibly bad idea. Adult children can be flaky, busy, financially burdened, child burdened, across the country, uninterested, physically disabled, mentally ill, dead, in conflict with siblings, squabbling over inheritances, or unwilling to spend said inheritance on care, not to mention unwilling or unable to spend their own money on it.

REMOVING THE BLINDERS

As discussed in chapter 3, the fear mongers would have us believe we will all be destitute if we don't start having more babies now, but fear not! The childfree have about as much of a safety net in our society as their parenting peers. The net may have a few holes, but it is not beyond repair.

For the childfree especially, planning starts with getting smart about your money. If we are going to have a shortage of caregivers, we had better be able to get competitive with compensation. We can't wait for a political solution or assume there will be some safety net for us. There is no substitute for good advice, so sit down with a financial planner and plot a course. If you are feeling aggrieved at the idea of someone else looking over your finances, start with one of the many fine books and resources out there. David Bach's series—*Smart Women Finish Rich, Smart Couples Finish Rich*, and for us late bloomers, *Start Late, Finish Rich*—are a good place to get your feet wet. You can also check out Bach's free resources at www.finishrich.com.

Also, be sure to have your medical directives and will in order. To whom will your money go? Who will make health decisions if you are not able to? Do you want the plug pulled? If so, who will pull it? All that fun stuff! To get started on these issues, check out Suze Orman's *Insurance Kit* or *Will & Trust Kit*. There are many additional resources and free referrals on her Web site at www.suzeorman.com.

Children are not an insurance policy. An *insurance policy* is an insurance policy. Make sure you have the coverage you need to protect your retirement savings, including life insurance and long-term care insurance. Most of us are familiar with the role of life insurance, which provides for dependents and covers your expenses upon your death. However, a relatively new product available that you'll want to check out is long-term care insurance (LTC). This does not replace traditional medical insurance, but instead complements it to cover things like in-home care, assisted living, and nursing care. If it is purchased before the age of sixty-five, the average annual premium will run about $1,337, or $2,862 after sixty-five. On average, an LTC insurance policy purchased at age sixty-five and held until death pays out eighty-two cents on the dollar. (16) However, for lots of Americans, an additional $112 per month is a lot for something they feel they may never use, and after age sixty-five, when income is starting to go down, the $239 per month may not be do-able. With the uncertainty of the future of health care, you may also find that many companies are dropping this product from their menu, so do your research. However, the cost and hassle of LTC insurance may seem more worth the trouble after examining the cost of senior housing.

I have seen two schools of thought with regard to senior housing options. The first group of folks will have to be dragged out of their house and into the retirement home (provided there is one) kicking and screaming, and the second group thinks that with its three square meals, laundry and maid service, "the home" sounds pretty good. The facts and figures, however, may be a bit shocking.

Let's say you are the type that thinks being in your own home as long as possible would be the preferred route. What most people do is wait until they have some debilitating event, like a broken hip, before even thinking about accessibility issues. If you don't have a lot of family or other advocates around, it may be too late to make the changes you need to stay in your home. However, you can plan to make your home accessible well before you need it. For many, the term "accessible" conjures pictures of long wheelchair ramps and ugly bars everywhere. But today the implementation of universal access is growing. These building modifications are unique because they can be used by anyone, disabled or not; are barely noticeable; and can actually add value to your home. In fact, if you are planning to remodel your home and hope to stay in that home as you age, talk to an aging-in-place specialist about universal access regardless of your current age or health status. The National Aging in Place Council has some good starter information at www.naipc.org.

Currently, aging-in-place specialists are helping seniors pay for costly modifications with home equity loans or, more commonly, reverse mortgages. If you're not familiar with the term, a reverse mortgage is a financial product wherein seniors sixty-two or older receive tax-free income based on the value of their home to use as they see fit. There are no mortgage payments, and the loan becomes repayable when the borrower sells the asset or moves out permanently. The repayment amount cannot exceed the value of the house, of course, so long-term planning and using caution when cashing out equity is essential to having this option.

During the housing boom of the early 2000s, we saw many people cash out equity for travel, schooling, home improvements, and so forth. Depending on how long the housing slump lasts, it may be some time before these same people rebuild any equity, making the tens of thousands of dollars needed for universal access modifications unavailable.

While there still seems to be a lot of pride wrapped around staying at home as one ages, and fear about "the home" for current retirees and even baby boomers, younger people I talk to seem to be less resistant to the idea of a more congregate setting. We'll see how and if that changes over time, but many Generation Xers I spoke with had little attachment to their houses and saw themselves in some sort of retirement community rather than home alone. Both options have pros and cons, but when I hear people of modest means with little or no retirement savings say, "I guess I'll probably end up in a home," I wonder if they have any idea what that really means or costs.

There are several different types of senior housing, with all different levels of care, depending on your wants and needs. Here is the lowdown that will put "the home" into perspective:

Retirement Communities – Apartments, condominiums, or houses in community settings for people age fifty-five or older. There are no personal care or meal services, but they may have social activities or local transportation options. Much will depend on location and individual need. Average monthly cost: $500–$4,000+. (17)

Independent Living – Much like retirement communities, these are unlicensed facilities that are age-restricted but provide congregate meals, transportation, social activities, and onsite management. Residents generally have a small room or apartment with bathroom and kitchen. Average monthly cost: $500–$4,000+. (18)

Assisted Living – These facilities offer an environment similar to independent living, except that they often limit or outright ban in-room cooking and may not have kitchens. Smaller assisted living facilities are referred to as "adult foster care" or "board and care." Usually, they have only a small handful of residents and are run out of someone's home. Assisted living facilities are state licensed to provide some basic additional care if needed. This would include things like bathing, dressing, and medication management. However, no major medical services are offered at this level, and unless you have long-term care insurance, all fees will need to be fully paid out of pocket. Average monthly cost: $2,500–$4,000+. (19)

Nursing Home – Licensed at the state level as well, nursing homes offer all the services of assisted living plus nursing and medical care. The nursing home is the one everyone usually wants to avoid, because at this level of care, functioning has severely deteriorated. There are two types of nursing homes: Intermediate Care Facilities (ICF), which require eight hours a day of nursing supervision; and Skilled Nursing Facilities (SNF), with round-the-clock nursing supervision. Generally, residents have a bed rather than a room. Some elderly who would benefit from the lower level of care provided in an assisted living facility end up here because it is the only option Medicare presently pays for. Average monthly cost: $3,000–$8,000+. (20)

Continuing Care Retirement Communities – This is your one-stop shop and my personal favorite. In CCRCs, you will find independent living, assisted living, and skilled nursing care all on the same campus. Most have a one-time buy-in fee and then charge an ongoing monthly rate. CCRCs agree to provide services for life and negate the need to move between various facilities as health deteriorates. Buy-in fees range from

$60,000–$400,000 or more. Average monthly cost after buy-in is $2,600 or more. (21)

All of these estimates are based on averages and not what is actually available today if you went out to find housing for an elderly person. Also, if you live in California, for example, the average will be higher than if you live in Ohio, so the low end of the spectrum does not apply to every community. My guess is that the low end won't apply to any community in the near future. As more seniors age and services become stretched, costs will go up—it's basic supply and demand.

So, if you are forgoing the $180,000 to $1,000,000 (22) a head it costs to have children, as discussed in chapter 4, how many "un-children" do you need to have to pay for old age? You are already more financially free than your parenting counterpart. Take the next step and insure your own future. None of us can count on government programs, pensions, Medicare, and so forth to be there in the quantity we may need, so it is up to us to be responsible and plan.

Parents in our culture often say they don't want to burden their children in old age. We don't want to burden the collective children of the future in old age, be it nieces, nephews, or society at large.

STAYING CONNECTED

Financial planning, housing, and health care are not the only concerns as we age, though. Remember that old lady shuffling across the street with her cart? To whom does she talk? With whom does she socialize? Where does she spend the holidays? Social connections are important at any age, but as we get older they are increasingly important, even precious.

Danielle, thirty-nine, has given the social network some priority and even thought beyond retirement to the potentiality of outliving her husband. *"I do think about who's going to take care of me when I get old, but not in the sense of who's actually physically doing it. Instead, I think,* Who am I going to grow old with over the long term? *Joe keeps saying he's not going to outlive me. I'm more concerned about my chosen family, otherwise known as my friends, than having kids so I won't be alone. I wouldn't want to put that burden on anybody, especially kids."*

Andrea, forty-five, is also building relationships with extended family for that reason. *"I think if you have a kid they may feel obligated to take care of you, and maybe they should, but in practice they really become more of a spokesperson for you. I think about my sister's three kids and say I'd better be pretty nice to them so that they'll speak up for me when I get old."*

The role adult children most frequently play with their aging parents is that of advocate. An advocate is someone who can speak for an ailing senior who is in a health crisis and unable to fully understand his or her rights and options. The advocate interacts with doctors, nurses, and hospital social services to ensure the right kind of care is being provided. The more social connections (i.e., friends) we have, the more likely someone will be asking questions on our behalf before, during, and, most important, after any type of long-term care is arranged.

Louise, thirty-nine, is a speech therapist in a hospital setting and has seen firsthand how unavailable for direct care adult children often are, but how important their advocacy still can be. *"I think a lot of people know the reality is that if your kids have kids they don't have a lot of time. They're working hard enough to be able to take care of themselves, let alone a parent. The important thing really is advocacy. What I've seen in the health-care system is that those people who are in crisis and have an advocate do better than those who don't. It is so very important, whether it's through friends, conservatorship, or whatever."*

If you don't have extended family to talk over end-of-life issues, or prefer not to go there with them, then the final part of your planning must be to designate an advocate for yourself, to manage your estate and medical decisions should something happen to you. In America, these advocates come in the form of conservators, both public and private. A public conservator, also referred to as a guardian, is usually assigned to seniors who are no longer able to take care of themselves and have no one to take responsibility for them. But you can plan ahead and choose your own advocate long before it comes to that. Usually, a durable power of attorney is the tool used to appoint someone you know and trust to handle your affairs in the event of your incapacitation. However, private conservators are another option, should you prefer to keep these arrangements separate from friends and family relationships. These people are often attorneys and are governed by state law, so check out your state's Web site for more information. I think choosing that person for yourself ahead of time—be it a family member, friend, or private conservator—is the best and most proactive route.

The best-laid plans are better than no plans, but still are no guarantee that your transition from this earth will be comfortable and smooth. The issues we will face in financing old age and getting the care we need affect all of us, regardless of whether or not we've produced offspring. The upside is that having kids isn't any more of a guarantee than not having them, so the argument that people should have kids in order to have someone to take care of them when they get old can be put to rest. Scott, forty-one, sums it up by saying, *"There's no guarantee that your kid is going to be there for you to take care of you when you get old. For our part, we're not any better off or worse off than our counterparts, and we're rolling the dice like everyone else. I'm a little bit concerned about Social Security not being there, but we're not depending on it anyway. By the time we retire, the working people versus the retiring people will probably be about one to one* [actually three to one]. *I have always dreamed about retiring to Mexico or someplace like that, where they have large expatriate communities of retired Americans, who are still getting along well in their older age, but are able to afford a better lifestyle. Now with the advent of the Internet you can probably live just about anywhere.*

There is no reason not to get creative and think outside the box. Kathleen, fifty-three, is one such creative thinker. *"I envision when I get old there will be lots of niche retirement homes. For example, my old theater friends from college—many of whom are gay and have no kids to take care of them—and I are going to all live in this house and do musical theater every night. We might not be doing the same show on the same night, but we're going to have a very good time! I have confidence that there are going to be so many of us that it will have to be tended to somehow."*

There will be lots of us, and necessity is the mother of invention. Like Kathleen, who envisions the niche retirement homes, Louise sees intentional communities as a possible solution. *"What I want to create are communities that come together with intentional people who are helping each other age gracefully. As many friends as I have who have children, I have as many who don't. There are going to be a lot of us, and we will have to figure out ways to take care of each other."*

Ultimately, the onus to educate and protect yourself is on you. Break through the cultural denial and realize that most likely you, too, will get old and incapacitated one day. That is not meant to scare you, but to inform you. The best way to make sure one of those elderly throwaways shuffling across the street is not you is to have a plan that goes beyond retirement planning and into old-age planning. There are no substitutes for educating yourself and, of course, good advice. Here's a piece: Do not have a child out of fear for the future. Children ≠ insurance.

7
You'll Regret It!

Don't waste life in doubts and fears; spend yourself on the work before you, well assured that the right performance of this hour's duties will be the best preparation for the hours and ages that will follow it.

—Ralph Waldo Emerson

The other night I went out for Thai food with friends. After we had overindulged in the best Southeast Asian cuisine I have had in a long time, the waitress came by to clear our plates and asked if we had saved room for dessert. "The special tonight is fried bananas with coconut ice cream." Yum! The last time I had that was on the island of Ko Samui. What could we do but order a plate? By the time I got home, my stomach was distended and my jeans were cutting off the blood flow between the upper and lower portions of my torso. Now, that I regret! But regret not having kids? I don't think so.

SCARED STRAIGHT

The ominous warning of "you'll regret it" can be grouped with similar arguments designed to wake us in the night trembling with fear at the prospect of being old and alone. Many of us are constantly deflecting coercions such as "it is different when they're your own," "you don't know what you're missing," or any of the other harangues covered in the six previous chapters. Perhaps we can be scared into procreating? After all, the utilization of fear tactics is effective for everything from selling wrinkle cream to preemptive wars. But unlike most things in life, once we have bought into parenthood, there's no way out. Not in four years, not in forty years, not ever. This is one life sentence that you have to be ready to serve, because as a wise friend once said to me, *"Having a child is like deciding to get a tattoo on your face. You'd better be really sure you want it!"*

The choice to become a parent is, for the most part, a permanent one, and regretting it is a pain with no remedy. A colleague of mine who has two small children said to me one day, "I don't know what I was thinking when I had children. My idea of what it would be like is so different from the reality. My best girlfriend tried to tell me, but I didn't want to listen to her. I wish I had!" Now, she does her best to be a good mother and she loves her children, but to admit such profound regret without offering some admonishment like "it's hard, but it's worth it" was a rare moment of honesty among women.

In my mid-twenties, I worked for a fifty-ish woman who overheard me telling a co-worker that I didn't want to have kids. She interrupted us with a diatribe on how lucky she thought I was, lamenting that if only such a choice had existed when she was a young woman, she never would have had children. "I hated being a mother!" she declared. I was blown away by her candor. Little did she know the profound impact that had on me. Her acknowledgment of my wisdom and good fortune made me feel as if I had figured out a secret that would save me from the regret of a lifetime. Thank you, wherever you may be!

Many childfrees have heard tales of regret from our parenting friends. Like Dave, fifty-one (aka Super Dave), we have been a safe harbor of understanding for them. *"I had a friend who really, really didn't want to have children, but his wife really did. So he finally caved in and had a child with her. He loves his daughter, who's almost grown at age seventeen, but he'll privately admit to me that he wishes he had made a different choice. The irony is that once they had the child, his wife wasn't a particularly good mother. Instead of being happy and fulfilled, like she thought she would be, she was less happy and less fulfilled. In fact, she was kind of a basket case. It made things even harder on my friend. I've heard a lot of parents admit they wish their lifestyle had been different or that they had made the decision not to have children. But obviously, once a child is there, you can't say, 'Poof! Go away!' Now it's a living, breathing human being. You can't be partway pregnant or sort of have kids. It's all or nothing. A lot of thought goes into being childfree. While many people get pregnant accidentally, no one doesn't get pregnant accidentally."*

The only people who come close to "accidentally" not getting pregnant are the unfortunate child*less* people out there who wanted children but didn't have a chance or couldn't because of health or fertility issues. It would be understandable and even expected that they feel loss or regret, and they deserve our compassion. In her groundbreaking book, *The Childless Revolution*, Madelyn Cain explores the reasons why 42 percent of women do not have children. She divides the non-mothers into three categories: choice, chance, and happenstance. There may be regrets, disappointment, and even grieving for the chance (health/fertility) and happenstance (opportunity) categories. Some women who are childless due to medical reasons, fertility problems, or financial and/or relationship instability have a lot of work to do to make peace with their non-parent status. However, with acceptance and support, these women can heal and channel their mother energy into other contributions. Still, many of us have seen the pain and suffering of friends and/or family who were either unable to conceive or unwilling to parent without a viable partner who never came along.

The childless by choice, on the other hand, are a completely different breed. Across the country, when talking to childfree people for this book, I heard resounding clarity and peace of mind regarding their decision. While I can concede that there may be a regretful childfree adult out there somewhere, I have yet to meet one in person. As Super Dave points out, the childfree give way too much consideration to their lifestyle decision to be plagued by regret.

A CHILDFREE'S PREROGATIVE

The closest thing I have found to a fear of regret among the childfree is a fear that they will change their mind. Perhaps fear isn't the right word, though, because while all of my interviewees were solidly childfree, they also were willing to look at the possibility of being suddenly hit with a case of baby rabies.

Lisa is single and twenty-six, and although she is very sure of her decision now, she admits, *"I do worry that I'll turn thirty and something will just click on, and suddenly I'll want to have a baby. I'll be honest about that. But I don't have a crystal ball and I can't see the future. At the same time, the issues I have now will be the same issues I'll have in my thirties. Those things would need to be considered first before I would even think about having children."*

Then there's Natalie, thirty-one and married for three years. She shares an experience common among many childfree women who are approaching an age when changing their minds is no longer a biological option. *"As I enter my thirties I do have a nagging fear that something's going to kick in and suddenly I'm going to want to have a baby. I constantly have to check myself. Do I still not want kids? No, I still don't want them. I tell myself that if I don't feel one hundred percent like I need to have children, I'm not going to have them, and I've never felt one hundred percent. Why would I have a kid if Tom and/or I weren't sure? Sometimes, I'll see a really cute kid from a distance and I'll think, 'Maybe. I mean, isn't she cute?' And then the next day at the grocery store, one of them will be screaming their head off and I'm snapped back. Nope, I don't want to do that. I do have some of those questioning moments, but the majority of the time it's a definite no."*

Andrea is a forty-five-year-old actress who also reexamined her desire to be childfree right when the clock started ticking down. In the end, she realized that her art is her baby and that's okay. *"When I entered perimenopause, there was a time of reexamining this issue on a deeper level. I have a lot of friends who, around age forty, had that baby panic, and went out and grabbed some random guy and had a kid. I didn't have any of that, but I wondered if, when I got older, I'd regret it. I have met people who never wanted to have kids but got pregnant by mistake, and afterward said,*

'Oh my gosh, I can't believe I almost didn't have a kid.' Then I looked at my honest reactions when I see a woman pushing a baby stroller down the street and my thoughts were, What a pain, *or I'd stay with my sister for a weekend and hang out with her three kids, and by the time I left I'd be thinking,* Oh, thank God I don't have kids. *I work very hard on my art. Artistic people often call their work their baby and I think in a lot of ways it is. I put that same level of nurturing into my work. So for me, it's hard to imagine adding something else that would require that level of energy, commitment, and attention."*

Lisa, Natalie, and Andrea are all willing to talk about the possibility of changing their minds. By staying conscious of it, they are coming to their decisions authentically rather than giving in to fear or social pressure. How many parents out there give their decision to *have* kids the same amount of thought?

Karen is thirty-five and has been living with her boyfriend for three years. She has been examining and reexamining her decision since the age of twenty. *"You can always change your mind if you're childfree. If you already have kids you can't. It's a big decision that we put a lot of thought into, and those of us who've chosen this lifestyle have really thought it through. Where some people have children accidentally when their birth control fails, this is definitely a chosen lifestyle. There's no way that I would have the time or the energy to put into raising a child the way I think it should be raised, and I planned my life accordingly. I don't think that people who have children put the same amount of thought into their choice as people who don't, and that bothers me a lot. Especially when people say that we are selfish."*

While conducting the ongoing examination that the childfree impose on their own lives, one other concern often surfaces. What if one day my partner changes his or her mind? In chapter 4 childfrees who had lost relationships over this issue shared their stories, and the conclusion was drawn that compromising on the issue of kids is impossible and certainly unfair to at least one partner. It is a legitimate issue that weighs on any childfree whose partner was ambivalent about having children and then agreed not to in order to be in the relationship.

Joe, forty, was never sure about having kids. *"I wasn't definite one way or the other. When I thought about it, it was more the fantasy thing of having a child to show things to and have fun with, but not the whole package. Then I met Danielle and I wanted to marry her, and it wasn't a pressing issue or desire for me. We talked about it before we moved in together and again before we got married."* Danielle always knew she didn't want to have kids and has been clear about that all along. Regardless, she admits, *"My biggest fear is that Joe will come home one day and say that he wants to have a child. I really don't know what I would do. I would go off the deep end."*

Alan's heart would also be broken if his partner changed her mind. *"I had a relationship with a woman that ended because she wanted to have kids. I cared for her and wanted her to be happy, so I let her go to find that happiness. Now I have been married for ten years to a woman who loves children but was ambivalent about having her own when we met. I feel like she gave up the option of being a mother to be with me, and if she ever decided she had to have that, I'd have to let her go, too. I love her too much to deny her that experience, but it can't be with me."*

The likelihood that a childfree will suddenly wake up at fifty years old and realize he or she should have had children is very slim, in light of the depth of consideration given to the subject. I would hope persons entering into a relationship with one of us would take the same time to consider their choice, and avoid deluding themselves with statements like, "She'll change her mind." She won't. Just like no one should have a baby to please someone else, no one should *not* have a baby to please someone else. When ambivalence strikes, perhaps it is helpful to remember what one wise childfree said: *"It's better to regret not having kids than it is to regret having them, because once they're here, they're here, and they are completely innocent in it all."*

Yes, the children of regretful parents are the innocent victims in it all. What happens when an adult regrets having children but is still legally and socially responsible for them? Surely, some of that regret gets taken out on the children in the form of impatience, criticism, emotional or physical abuse, lax parenting, and more. When parents unconsciously blame their children for robbing them of their true purpose, they may project all sorts of negativity onto their blameless offspring.

The reasons that people choose to parent or not are broad and not easily summarized. There are parents who thoroughly explore their decision to have children long before embarking on the journey, just as there are parents who have children without much thought at all. Either way, some end up fulfilled while others have regret. Then there are childless folks for whom nature, ambivalence, and/or the passage of time decided for them. Some of these people have resolved that eventuality and others regret not taking another road. So, while the reasons for or against and the outcomes of each cannot be summed up in a nice and tidy way, there is one generalization I feel pretty safe making. The childfree, while diverse in their reasoning, have contemplated this decision far too much for there to be a big risk of feeling regret. Most of us still are raised with the assumption that one grows up, gets married, and has children. If we follow along and do get married, the next question is *when*, not *if*, we are going to have kids. To break the social norms and swim against the currents of conventional wisdom requires a lot of self-awareness and courage. It is nearly impossible to intentionally forgo something so culturally expected as having children without a highly developed consciousness and perhaps some thick skin.

While having children is an irreversible decision, the choice not to be a parent is absolutely reversible at almost any age. Whether we have biological children, adopt children, or become involved in the lives of children as a foster parent, the option is always there for the childfree. Yet none of the childfrees I spoke with anticipate acting on those options any time soon.

For the childfree, parenthood is like a pair of skinny jeans hanging in the back of the closet. We could get back into them should the mood strike, but like that pair of skinny jeans, parenthood is not a good fit for us, and we know it. We even relish it.

WHAT WE'RE MISSING – OR NOT

While choosing not to have kids is a serious decision, that doesn't mean we can't have some fun with it. In her book *Baby Not on Board: A Celebration of Life without Kids,* Jennifer L. Shawne uses humor to illustrate the many joys of being childfree, and the many reasons we won't regret it. For Shawne, "Pamper" isn't a diaper, and she reaffirms the joy (and financial freedom) of being childfree. (1)

Shawne offers ten things you'll never be called upon to pay for (*italicized text added*):

1. Baby food musher *(until you're 80, at least)*
2. Preschool tuition *(except for your inner child—aka therapy bills)*
3. The latest must-have sneakers *(except to impress at the gym!)*
4. School or sports uniforms *(unless you have a weird fetish!)*
5. Ritalin prescription *(unless you have the attention span of a gnat!)*
6. Additional airplane seat *(unless you let yourself go!)*
7. Braces *(unless you look like Bugs Bunny!)*
8. Rock festival tickets *(unless you're still rockin'!)*
9. Prom night *(unless some drunk teenager sideswipes your new convertible!)*
10. College *(except when to do so fulfills your own educational dreams!)*

When I asked my interviewees if they thought there was anything they might miss out on by not having kids, the most common replies were things like, *"Yeah, I'll miss years of dirty diapers,"* or *"I'll miss staying up all night worrying."* Or as Meagn, forty-nine, said, *"The only thing I miss by not having kids is that ever-elusive societal approval. You know, everyone thinking you're so great because you're a mother. For some reason, that seems to be the 'get out of jail free' card for women. It instantly attaches some sort of credibility to you, whether you deserve it or not."*

While some childfrees may have never considered parenthood as one of the infinite possibilities in life, others do acknowledge that there are things they might miss, but not regret, about their choice. Just as it is hard for a parent to admit regret about having a child, it can be difficult for a childfree to admit there may be things they are missing out on, other than the high price of braces and college tuition. Such admissions, though, are actually more evidence of a mature, well thought out decision.

Viki, twenty-nine, may miss having adult children as friends. *"I know my mom really enjoys having adult children. We had a cookout here on Memorial Day and had a very good time sitting and chatting. That would be the kind of thing I'll miss out on."*

Kathy, fifty-one, is finding new ways to enjoy the holidays. *"The trade-off is at Christmastime, when everyone has his or her big families to go to. Then there's what to do for Thanksgivings and things like that. But I realize it's not so much about having kids as not having a lot of family around. As an only child, I don't have siblings, or nieces and nephews, either. The holidays are the one time that it seems a little weird. But we have figured out how to make the best of it. For example, last Easter we took the RV and went on a camping trip to Hershey Park. During the holidays, I also hear a lot of people talking about family strife, and how they haven't talked to this brother or that sister in years, and it makes me remember that just because you have family doesn't mean you're going to be close."*

Nicole, thirty-eight, knows what she's missing—and isn't missing it! *"It seems like lately I'm in these situations where I'm surrounded by women who all have children. When they ask, 'Do you have kids?' and I say no, they reply, 'I'm sorry.' That really catches me off guard. I'm not sorry at all, so why should you be? I went to a scrapbooking event where everyone else was a mother. They kept talking about their kids and I couldn't participate in the conversation at all. I tried to change the subject a few times, but it didn't work very well. Those kinds of conversations are boring. I mean, what else do you do? I called my husband as soon as I left and said, 'Honey, I'm so glad we are us. I could never do that.' Sure, by not having kids, you miss those moments—key word being 'moments'—like first words and grabbing your finger for the first time. But then there's all the time in between the moments! Problem is, if you admit to a fleeting moment where you think,* Maybe I can have a child, *people think that deep down inside you must really want one. But it's not true. I think more about the long-term enjoyment I have in my life and not only the little moments that I'm missing out on. I think of all the great moments we have, and there are so many things I can't even count them all. Then, if we do want to be involved in children's lives somehow, we can do that, because we don't have our own."*

The postcard moments Nicole mentions are the window dressing that pulls at some of our heartstrings, but that does not mean the childfree are in denial and secretly want to have babies. A few months before I began this project in earnest, a very good friend of mine had her first baby. She shared with me how moving it was to be in the delivery room when her son arrived. *"It is the only time I have ever seen David cry, and he bawled almost as much as the baby! We both did. It was such a bonding for us."* How incredible it would be to share such a powerful experience. It is easy to forget that to have that experience you would also have to go through pregnancy and childbirth, and raise a child for twenty years or more.

Perhaps it is the draw of sharing this intense moment, forming the bonds similar to those of soldiers in battle that tempts partners in rocky relationships to have a baby in order to "fix it." Certainly, the idealized version of childbirth seen in so many television shows and movies fills the collective imagination of potential parents far more than the reality that comes after.

Being aware that you are missing something is different from regretting what you have. Feeling a pang of envy when a friend relays a "precious moment" story doesn't mean your decision not to have kids was wrong. Because the childfree life is still marginalized in our society, such pangs can lead to fear, doubt, and indecision. Remember that plenty of parents hear about our childfree life and envy our freedom. That doesn't necessarily mean they made the wrong decision for themselves, either. I know that no matter how many beautiful baby moments reach my ears, I always return to a place of certainty about my decision. If it is the right decision for you, you will, too.

For the childfree, once we have made peace with our decision it is unshakable. We are 100 percent sure of ourselves, but convincing others of our certainty can be a different story.

Alison is already very sure of her desire to be childfree. However, at twenty-four years old, she has had experience with many a naysayer challenging her position. *"The people who are unsupportive are the ones who have children, who are older and say things that are really patronizing like, 'You'll change your mind when you're twenty-nine' or 'You'll feel differently later.' And these are the experiences that really offend me the most. I understand that I still have a lot of developing to do in my life, but to say that I don't understand something as fundamental as this is extraordinarily insulting. It is like saying, 'Oh, you've chosen the wrong job; you need to quit your job and go do something different, but you'll figure it out eventually.' No one would ever say that to you, but when it comes to something more profound, like the decision not to have a child, everyone thinks they get to have an opinion. I don't think that anything could be more insulting. Sometimes I don't even tell people I don't want kids because I don't want to deal with that look that says, 'Oh, okay, sure you don't, wait till your ovaries start screaming.' It's easier to not address it."*

It is certainly far less important to convince others of the validity of your decision than it is to be sure of it yourself. If you are certain, no amount of browbeating from anyone will diminish your resolve. If you are doing it for the wrong reasons, like to save a relationship or fulfill someone else's worldview, then regret is a real possibility. I can't stress enough the importance of getting clear on this in your own mind and heart, whether it is by reading books or talking to a counselor or seeking other advice. Childfrees often recognize parenthood as one of many roads not taken in this life, and yet they are very comfortable with the paths they are on.

Sandi, forty-eight, says, *"No regrets. I love the life John and I are leading right now. What's perfect for some people isn't perfect for everyone. I appreciate people who have children, because we need a few around. I enjoy seeing them around the neighborhood and watching them grow, but I don't need to have them myself. I am accompanying John on a business trip to Scotland in a few months, and that is one of the many things I would regret missing if I did have kids."*

Eileen, forty-eight, states, *"I don't see any negatives in my decision not to have children. It has been nothing but positive for me. In fact, I look around at women only a little bit older than I am and many of them are raising their grandchildren. They don't ever get a break. Not having children has been one of the biggest decisions of my life and has colored everything else. I am a very happy childfree person. I have no regrets."*

Janet, forty-four, comments, *"I used to fear that I would regret it, but not anymore. I have this philosophy of life where I believe in reincarnation; not in the 'I used to be Joan of Arc' way, but I do get a sense that we get to go around again. I can't really fully articulate it, but I guess I don't feel like I have to do everything in this life. I look at my elderly aunts and uncles who have grown kids in trouble with drugs or the law and I wonder what comfort that brought them. I think once you make the decision and you are at peace with it, it's the best thing ever. It is so freeing and so great. This is what feminism is all about—having options and making choices, not simply doing things because you are obligated by society. The same thing goes for men, too."*

Vicki, forty-six, says, *"Going into menopause, many empty nesters are wondering how to create meaning in their lives, but I feel like I've been filling my life with meaning all along. I do not worry about regretting my decision at all. My husband and I look at each other and we're really so grateful and so thrilled that we made this decision. Our lives are so full, and I know I will never regret it."*

Friends, family, co-workers, and even perfect strangers may still feel emboldened to question your decision and challenge your determination. Even if there is no one challenging you on a regular basis, society at large persists in spreading around the conventional wisdom that you should grow up, get married, and have children. It is not hard to see, then, why we may even question ourselves. Yet none of the age-old objections—including accusations of selfishness, obligations to society or religion, letting down parents, not being cared for in old age, and so on—have stood up to scrutiny. By debunking these unsound objections you are able to follow your own path, free from internal doubts and armed against external ones.

Should you decide to become or continue to be childfree, you are not alone! There is strong community support for your wise, well-thought-out decision. On the other hand, if after thoughtful reflection you choose to become a parent, know that many of us in the childfree community will be happy to support you in raising a well-adjusted member of society. Both parents and childfrees have a place at the social negotiating table, and by respecting the choices each makes, we can forge a trail to a healthier and more sustainable existence. Whatever path you choose, be sure to enjoy the journey.

Epilogue
Now What? Finding Your Childfree Purpose.

And the day came when the risk to remain tight in a bud was more painful than the risk it took to blossom.

—Anaïs Nin

I am sitting in an outdoor hot tub gazing at the stars. It is a clear night, and the moon is closing in on full, reflecting off the fresh snowdrifts that surround us. I can hear the Deschutes River rolling by, smoothing the craggy rocks that haplessly attempt to impede her powerful flow.

I have dropped everything to come visit my sister, who just adopted a baby. Spontaneous travel to support family, yet another freedom of the childfree!

For everyone's sanity, I am staying in a hotel near her home in beautiful central Oregon. Through the sliding glass door I can see the indoor pool and spa swarming with kids ranging in age from three to thirteen. Although the door is closed, I can still hear the shrieking that tells me the noise inside must be deafening to the exhausted-looking parents who sit slumped in the surrounding chairs. Still clad in their winter coats, they tolerate the eighty-degree room, dutifully minding their rambunctious offspring.

I wonder how I could be so lucky. Each and every day that passes, I am awestruck by the many joys in my life. These are the moments when I really relish being childfree.

Choosing a life without children is not merely about going against the grain, making a statement about society, or pointing out all of the annoyances of megalomaniacal parents. It is about creating a life that honors your dreams, your vision, and your purpose. In life we play many roles, which give us a sense of what to do, but they are not true being or fulfillment of purpose. Many roles, like husband, wife, and parent give us a sense of identity, yet these roles in particular are based on another person, not our true self.

For much of my young life, my own identity was defined by the things I *didn't* want, as opposed to the things I *did* want. I *didn't* want to be trapped in a traditional marriage. I *didn't* want to work in a soul-sucking corporate job. I *didn't* want to be a full-time babysitter to my offspring. As a result, I had relationships with unavailable (emotionally or geographically) men, lost or quit every job I had, and denied my own innate creativity until it finally made me physically ill.

In October 2007 I was diagnosed with a condition called endometriosis, a malady wherein intrauterine tissue grows outside the uterus, wreaking all sorts of havoc on the reproductive system and often growing into cysts that are sized on the fruit scale—apples, melons, and so on. While this condition is fairly common, it affects childless women at much higher rates. There is no known cause for endometriosis, and while it can be painful and disruptive, it is not life-threatening.

The irony of having two large cysts, together the size of a growing fetus, removed from my ovaries in a surgery that left me with what looks like a C-section scar, all while writing a book for and about the childfree, is not lost on me. However, my awareness of the mind-body connection has been broadened to such a degree that I now believe that no matter what physical attributes led to this illness, the emotional and spiritual stagnation I had developed by avoiding life's "pitfalls" played a large role as well. So as I birth this project out into the world, it is with a new perspective on life that is far more focused on creating the life I want—not just avoiding the one I don't. It may be harder for us, the childfree, because we don't have the benefit of generations before us who forged a path and showed us what is possible. We have to forge that path ourselves and be the example so that others who follow can finally see parenting as one choice of many and make plans based on facts, not fear. It is my deepest hope that you will take a moment to reflect on what you, as a childfree adult, want to "birth" in this life and whether you are giving yourself permission to do so. It may be as simple as birthing your true, authentic self.

There are so many perks to being childfree that it is hard not to sound like a cheerleader for the cause. Be it weekends spent alone, traveling during the peace and quiet of the off-season, or never having to sit through Disney's *Snow Dogs*, there's much to be grateful for. Perhaps the greatest gift my childfree life gives me is the opportunity for personal development.

The task of parenting gives some of our peers an instant life purpose, whether by accident or thoughtful choice. The childfree must find and create their own great challenges, be they building a business, excelling in a chosen career, or dedicating ourselves to our art, passion, or a humanitarian cause.

For Vicki, forty-six, it is vulnerable children and teens that get her involved. *"There is an organization in downtown Detroit called COTS, Coalition on Temporary Shelter, where I participated in some of the holiday events, delivering toys, managing the toy room. I even took a group of kids to a Tigers baseball game last year. I've been working with a woman here who founded an organization called 'Reaching Higher.' The purpose of Reaching Higher is to reach at-risk youth with an eight-week class to boost their self-esteem and let them know they are special in the world. It gives them a safe place to open up, where they might not be able to do that at home."* In addition, Vicki is continuing to learn and grow professionally, with plans to leave her nine-to-five job and build her own business. *"In my early forties, I got into Pilates for some relaxation and a good way to exercise. I was instantly hooked, so I enrolled in the program for becoming an instructor. Now I have a side business out of my house teaching one-on-one Pilates. I've met some wonderful people and it's opened up a new world for me. I'm entering the second half of my life really energized, knowing that I can leave the automotive industry in the next few years and be teaching Pilates. That is my long-term goal. I feel like in a lot of respects I'm only beginning. I am able to pursue a new career because I don't have anything holding me back."*

Louise, thirty-nine and free from parenting constraints, has nurtured relationships and contributed to the community. *"I've had all of these wonderful experiences and relationships that I wouldn't have had if I had made a different choice. It's a trade-off. I won't have grandchildren, but I do have a deeper relationship with my husband than most parents I know. I've been able to give back to the community as a hospice volunteer for years, and end-of-life issues are very important to me. I've also been volunteering with 'Dress for Success,' which provides professional clothing and coaching to women who are reentering the workforce. I'm a volunteer with the Oregon Food Bank, I have taken days off work to go plant trees, and done all sorts of things in the community that I wouldn't have been able to do if I'd had children."*

My dear friend Kathleen went from being childless to childfree by realizing that her gift to us all as a minister and spiritual advisor was her "baby." *"I used to sometimes wonder, in my moments of despair, why I was born a woman if I wasn't going to have children. But I know now that I am here to give birth in many ways. Babies still show up in my dreams, but I interpret them symbolically. The other night I was dreaming that I was at someone's house and I forgot that I was supposed to be taking care of the baby. Once I remembered, I went into the baby's room, and I wasn't sure if it was dead or alive. I was thinking,* Please don't be cold, please don't be cold. *I touched it, and it was warm and alive. Babies in dreams are a metaphor for other things I am symbolically giving birth to, not literally, and they, too, are warm and alive. We all have the ability to birth and create, including men. Some of us are here to do it literally, while others are here to do it symbolically, creatively, or energetically."*

Shannon, thirty-five, grew up in a home with very traditional values and channels her nurturing energies to friends, neighbors, and peers. *"Because I am a parent to no one, I am a parent to all. I am able to be a positive influence in the lives of the children around me, be they nieces, nephews, friends, or neighbors. The neighborhood kids used to call me the 'Kool-Aid mom,' even though I'm not a parent. They would come over and help me outside and whatnot. I am a lot less stressed and drained than many of the adults I am around, which makes it possible for me to be a positive support to them. I have also always been very involved in my church, and usually it has been in the singles outreach or singles ministries because I have some expertise there. Many times, spiritual organizations will forget about the unmarried or those who don't have children because they are focusing on the growth and furthering of the church, which is most easily done with people's children. I help them to feel included."*

So, while you are blazing the trail of the childfree—exploring, inventing, or just being—don't forget to have some fun and laugh along the way. No matter what foolish or silly things others may say about your choice, be confident in knowing that their protests stem from their fear and doubt, not yours. Your purpose lies elsewhere, and that is beautiful.

My purpose is not only to take the heat on behalf of my fellow childfrees, but to educate our families and peers on the validity and value inherent in our choice. I dream of the day that the old mantra of "when you grow up, get married, and have kids" is replaced by "when you grow up, if you decide to get married and if you choose to have kids." I want young men and women everywhere to see parenting as a choice, understand their options, and only then act in accordance with their wants and desires. I know there are young people out there right now who have never been told that having children is optional. Perhaps they are questioning themselves and wondering if their lack of interest in having children means they are somehow broken. But the only thing that is broken is the old conventional wisdom that wanting children is "normal" and not wanting them is "abnormal." Trust your inner wisdom, don't give in to fear, and follow your heart and your dreams, knowing that by doing so you set an example for the next guy or gal.

I will follow my own advice and continue forward by focusing on what I want, as opposed to what I don't want. Wonderful friends, a healthy family and meaningful work are all things I have or want. Now I am finding a broader sense of purpose by giving voice to an invisible and ignored group of people in order to build fellowship and tell our stories.

For more information about upcoming projects, please visit my Web site at **www.karenfoster.net**. I look forward to our continued dialogue.

Notes

Introduction

1. United States v. One Package 1936.
2. Griswold v. Connecticut 1965.
3. Eisenstat v. Baird 1972.
4. Chandra, A., G.M. Martinez, W.D. Mosher, J.C. Abma, and J. Jones, "Fertility, Family Planning, and Reproductive Health of U.S. Women: Data from the 2002 National Survey of Family Growth." National Center for Health Statistics, *Vital Health Stat 23(25)*. 2005.
5. Ibid.
6. Finer, Lawrence B. and Stanley K. Henshaw, "Disparities in Rates of Unintended Pregnancy in the United States, 1994 and 2001," *Perspectives on Sexual and Reproductive Health*, Vol. 38, No. 2 (June 2006), pp. 90–96, Guttmacher Institute.

Chapter 1

1. Bianco, Robert, "Baby Borrowers: Shame on NBC Adults," *USA Today*, June 24, 2008.
2. Finer, Lawrence B. and Stanley K. Henshaw, "Disparities in Rates of Unintended Pregnancy in the United States, 1994 and 2001," *Perspectives on Sexual*

and Reproductive Health, Vol. 38, No. 2 (June 2006), pp. 90–96, Guttmacher Institute.

3. Friedman, Carrie, "Stop Setting Alarms on My Biological Clock," *Newsweek*, July 2007.

4. Gilbert, Daniel, *Stumbling on Happiness*, Vintage Books, 2005, p. 243.

5. Evenson, J. Ranae and W. Robin Simon, "Clarifying the Relationship between Parenthood and Depression," *Journal of Health and Social Behavior* 2005, Vol 46 (December): 341–358.

6. Gilbert, Daniel, *Stumbling on Happiness*, Vintage Books, 2005, p. 244.

7. United Nations, Department of Economic and Social Affairs, Population Division, "World Population Prospects: The 2006 Revision, Highlights, Working Paper No. ESA/P/WP.202." 2007.

8. Couvrette, Phil, "Teen With Peanut Allergy Dies After Kiss; Girl's Boyfriend Had Just Eaten Peanut Butter Snack, Officials Say," *Associated Press*, November 28, 2005.

9. Couvrette, Phil, "Teen Died From Asthma Attack, Not From Peanut Butter Kiss, Coroner Says," *Associated Press*, May 11, 2006.

10. Gilbert, Carol Bengle, "Peanut Allergy and School Bans on Peanut Products: Sound Policy or Hysteria?" *Associated Content*, October 26, 2007.

11. Nevius, C.W., "One 5-Year-Old's Allergy Leads to Class Peanut Ban: Dozens of Parents at PTA Meeting Question Lunch Searches, Nurse," *San Francisco Chronicle*, September 9, 2003.

12. H.R.1523 Introduced by Representative Edward Marke, D-MA, March 16, 2009, S. 593 Introduced by Senator Diane Feinstein, D-CA, March 12, 2009. For current status see www.govtrack.us.

13. Nord, Mark, M. Andrews, S. Carlson. "Household Food Security in the United States," *United States Department of Agriculture/Economic Research Service*, 2007.

14. Douglas-Hall, Ayana, Michelle Chau, and Heather Koball, "Basic Facts About Low-Income Children, Birth to Age 18," *National Center for Children In Poverty*, September 2006.

15. DeNavas-Walt, Carmen, Bernadette D. Proctor, and Jessica Smith, "Income, Poverty, and Health Insurance Coverage in the United States: 2006," U.S. Census Bureau, *Current Population Reports*, pp. 60–233, U.S. Government Printing Office, Washington, DC, 2007.

16. MacDorman, M.F. and T.J. Mathews, "Recent Trends in Infant Mortality in the United States," *NCHS Data Brief*, no 9. Hyattsville, MD: National Center for Health Statistics. 2008.

17. Nathan Thornburgh/Shelbyville, "Dropout Nation," *Time* Magazine, Sunday, April 09, 2006.

18. Fox, Maggie, "Medical Bills Underlie 60 Percent of U.S. Bankruptcies – U. S. Study," Reuters, June 4, 2009.

19. Fox, Maggie, "Half of Bankruptcy Due to Medical Bills – U.S. Study," Reuters, February 2, 2005.

20. Fox, Maggie, "Medical Bills Underlie 60 Percent of U.S. Bankruptcies – U. S. Study," Reuters, June 4, 2009.

21. U.S. Department of the Treasury, www.treasurydirect.gov, June 25, 2009.

22. U.S. Census Bureau, www.census.gov, June 27, 2009.

23. Brown, Ansel, Lisa James, Kathleen Keest, Jabrina Robinson, and Ellen Schloemer, "The Plastic Safety

Net: The Reality Behind Debt in America," Report by Demos and Center for Responsible Lending, October 2005.

Chapter 2
1. Image Archive on the American Eugenics Movement, "Ethical, Legal and Social Implications Research Program," National Human Genome Research Institute.
2. Ibid.
3. Centers for Disease Control and Prevention, American Society for Reproductive Medicine, Society for Assisted Reproductive Technology, "2006 Assisted Reproductive Technology Success Rates: National Summary and Fertility Clinic Reports," Atlanta: U.S. Department of Health and Human Services, Centers for Disease Control and Prevention; 2008.
4. Ibid.
5. Centers for Disease Control and Prevention, "National Birth Defects Prevention Study Shows Assisted Reproductive Technology is Associated with an Increased Risk of Certain Birth Defects," U.S. Department of Health and Human Services, November 17, 2008.
6. Centers for Disease Control and Prevention, American Society for Reproductive Medicine, Society for Assisted Reproductive Technology,. "2006 Assisted Reproductive Technology Success Rates: National Summary and Fertility Clinic Reports," Atlanta: U.S. Department of Health and Human Services, Centers for Disease Control and Prevention; 2008.

7. March of Dimes, "Multiples: Twins, Triplets and Beyond, Quick Reference Fact Sheet," March 2009.

8. American Society for Reproductive Medicine, "Complications of Multiple Gestation," Patient's Fact Sheet, 2001.

9. Swamy, Geeta K., M.D., Turls Ostbye, M.D., and Rolv Skjaerven, PhD., "Association of Preterm Birth With Long-term Survival, Reproduction, and Next-Generation Preterm Birth", *Journal of the American Medical Association*, Vol. 299 (12), March 26, 2008.

10. U.S. Department of Health and Human Services, "HHS Launches New Campaign to Encourage Adoption of Children from Foster Care," News Release, July 15, 2004.

11. Lake, Ricki, *The Business of Being Born*, New Line Home Video, May 6, 2008.

12. Ibid.

13. Ibid.

14. Ibid.

15. Ibid.

16. Ibid.

17. Ibid.

18. Ibid.

19. Ibid.

20. Park, Alice, "Baby Einsteins: Not So Smart After All," *Time* Magazine, August 6, 2007.

21. Ibid

22. Rosin, Hanna, "The Case Against Breast Feeding," *The Atlantic,* April 2009.

23. Bennett, Laura, "My War Against Food Nazi Moms," *The Daily Beast,* January 3, 2009.

24. "Building a Dream – The Oprah Winfrey Leadership Academy," Harpo, Inc., 2007.

25. Edmonds, Patricia, "Oprah's Greatest Gift," *USA Weekend* Magazine, December 17, 2009.

Chapter 3

1. "Field Listing: Total Fertility Rate, The World Factbook," Central Intelligence Agency, 2009.
2. Kher, Unmesh, "Oceans of Nothing," *Time* Magazine, November 5, 2006.
3. Worm, Boris, et al., "Impacts of Biodiversity Loss on Ocean Ecosystem Services," *Science*, Vol. 314 (5800) pp. 787–790, November 3, 2006.
4. Thomas, Chris D. et al., "Feeling the Heat, Climate Change and Biodiversity Loss," *Nature*, 427 pp. 145–148, January 8, 2008.
5. Wilson, Edward O., *The Future of Life*, Vintage Books, 2002.
6. Tremlett, Giles, "Global Warming to Wash Away Beaches, Warns Spanish Study," *Guardian*, September 11, 2006.
7. Gore, Al, *An Inconvenient Truth: The Planetary Emergency of Global Warming and What We Can Do About It*, Rodale Books, May 26, 2006.
8. Netherland Environmental Assessment Agency, "China Now No. 1 in CO_2 Emissions; USA in Second Position," Press Release, June 19, 2007.
9. Michael R. Raupach, et al., "Global and Regional Drivers of Accelerating CO_2 Emissions," *Proceedings of the National Academy of Sciences of the United States of America (PNAS)*, April 17, 2007.
10. U.S. Bureau of the Census, International Data Base, www.census.gov/ipc/www/ibd/index.php.

11. Shorto, Russell, "No Babies?" *New York Times Magazine,* June 29, 2008.
12. Ibid.
13. Blankley, Tony, "The McLaughlin Group," Federal News Services, Inc. Comments originally aired September 14, 2007.
14. Buchanan, Patrick J., *The Death of the West: How Dying Populations and Immigrant Invasions Imperil Our Country and Civilizations,* St. Martin's Griffin, 2002.
15. U.S. Bureau of the Census, "Vital Statistics of the United States," National Center for Health Statistics, 2004.
16. Ibid.
17. Prepared For Rep. Henry A. Waxman, "The Content Of Federally Funded Abstinence-Only Education Programs", United States House Of Representatives, Committee On Government Reform — Minority Staff, Special Investigations Division, December 2004.
18. Ibid.
19. Ibid.
20. Maher, Bill, *Bill Maher: The Decider,* HBO Home Video, November 20, 2007.
21. Boodman, Sandra G., "Virginity Pledges Can't Be Taken on Faith," *Washington Post,* May 16, 2006.
22. Ibid.
23. Ibid.
24. U.S. Department of Health and Human Services, *National Vital Statistics Reports,* Vol. 56, No. 7, National Center for Health Statistics, December 5, 2007.
25. Ibid.

26. American Psychological Association, "Based on the Research, Comprehensive Sex Education Is More Effective at Stopping the Spread of HIV Infection, Says APA Committee," Media Information, February 23, 2005.

27. Howell, Marcella, updated 2007 by Marilyn Keefe, "The History of Federal Abstinence-Only Funding," Advocates for Youth, July 2007.

28. Kehrl, Brian H., "States Abstain from Federal Sex Ed Money," Stateline.org, November 29, 2005.

29. Population Division of the Department of Economic and Social Affairs of the United Nations Secretariat, "World Population Prospects: The 2006 Revision, Highlights," New York: United Nations 2007.

30. Joint United Nations Programme on HIV/AIDS, "2008 Report on the Global AIDS Epidemic" *INAIDS*, August 2008.

31. State of the World Population 2005, "Reproductive Health: A Measure of Equity" UNFPA, 2005.

32. Report to Congressional Committees, "Health Spending Requirement Presents Challenges for Allocating Prevention Funding under the President's Emergency Plan for AIDS Relief," United States Government Accountability Office, April 2006.

Chapter 4

1. Chandra, A., G.M Martinez, W.D. Mosher, J.C. Abma, and J. Jones, "Fertility, Family Planning, and reproductive Health of U.S. Women: Data from the 2002 National Survey of Family Growth. National Center for Health Statistics." *Vital Health Stat* 23(25). 2005.

2. Fein, Ellen and Sherrie Schneider, *All The Rules: Time-tested Secrets for Capturing the Heart of Mr. Right*, p. 63, Warner Books, 2007.

3. Lyubomirsky, Sonja, *The How of Happiness: A New Approach to Getting the Life You Want*, p. 52, Penguin Books, 2007.

4. Giffin, Emily, *Baby Proof*, St. Martin's Griffin, p. 368, May 15, 2007.

5. U.S. Bureau of the Census, "Vital Statistics of the United States," National Center for Health Statistics, 2004.

6. Rosenstein, Edward, and Roger Weisberg "Waging a Living," Docurama, September 26, 2006.

7. Ibid.

8. Ibid.

9. Ibid.

10. Ibid.

11. DePaulo, Bella, Ph.D., *Singled Out: How Singles Are Stereotyped, Stigmatized, and Ignored, and Still Live Happily Ever After*, pp. 35, 41, St. Martin's Press, 2006.

12. U.S. Census Bureau, "The 2009 Statistical Abstract," 2009.

13. DePaulo, Bella, Ph.D., *Singled Out: How Singles Are Stereotyped, Stigmatized, and Ignored, and Still Live Happily Ever After*, p. 26, St. Martin's Press, 2006.

14. Center for Nutrition Policy and Promotion, "Expenditures on Children by Families, 2006," U.S. Department of Agriculture, April 2007.

15. Longman, Phillip, *The Empty Cradle: How Falling Birthrates Threaten World Prosperity and What to Do About It*, p. 73, A New America Book, Published by Basic Books, A Member of the Perseus Books Group, 2004.

Chapter 5
1. U.S. Census Bureau, "Grandparents Living With Grandchildren: 2000," Census 2000 Brief, October 2003.
2. Ibid.
3. Ibid.
4. Ibid.
5. Abram, J.C. and G. M. Martinez, "Childlessness Among Older Women in the United States: Trends and Profiles," *Journal of Marriage and Family*, (68)4:1045–1056, 2006.

Chapter 6
1. Sherman, Arloc, and Isaac Shapiro, "Social Security Lifts 13 Million Seniors Above the Poverty Line, A State-by-State Analysis," Center on Budget and Policy Priorities, February 24, 2005.
2. National Center for Health Statistics, *National Vital Statistics Reports*, vol. 54, no. 19, June 28, 2006.
3. Mathew Greenwald & Associates, Inc., "These Four Walls: Americans 45+ Talk about Home and Community," American Association of Retired Persons (AARP), May, 2003.
4. Ibid.
5. Ibid., p. 20.
6. United States House of Representatives Committee on Oversight and Government Reform, "Private Medicare Drug Plans: High Expenses and Low Rebates Increase the Costs of Medicare Drug Coverage," p. v, Majority Staff, October 2007.
7. Ibid.

8. The Caregiving Project for Older Americans, "Caregiving In America," International Longevity Center-USA, Ltd., 2006.
9. Ibid.
10. Ibid.
11. Ibid.
12. Ibid.
13. Ibid.
14. Ibid.
15. Ibid.
16. "Aging Services, The Facts," American Association of Homes and Services for the Aging (AAHSA), 2009.
17. What Happens Now: Senior Living, "What Types Of Senior Living Services Are Available?" What HappensNow.com, September 2008.
18. Ibid.
19. Ibid.
20. Ibid.
21. Ibid.

Chapter 7
1. Shawne, Jennifer, *Baby Not on Board*, Chronicle Books, 2005.

Bibliography

Bach, David, *Start Late, Finish Rich: A No Fail Plan for Achieving Financial Freedom at Any Age*, Broadway, 2007.

Bach, David, *Smart Women Finish Rich: 9 Steps to Achieving Financial Security and Funding Your Dreams*, Broadway, 2002.

Bach, David, *Smart Couples Finish Rich: 9 Steps for Creating a Rich Future for You and Your Partner*, Broadway, 2002.

Buchanan, Patrick J., *The Death of the West: How Dying Populations and Immigrant Invasions Imperil Our Country and Civilization*, New York, Thomas Dunne (St. Martin's Press), 2002.

Burkett, Elinor, *The Baby Boon: How Family-Friendly America Cheats the Childless*, New York, The Free Press, 2000.

Cain, Madelyn, *The Childless Revolution: What It Means to Be Childless Today*, New York, Perseus Publishing, 2001.

Carroll, Laura, *Families of Two: Interviews with Happily Married Couples without Children by Choice*, Xlibris Corporation, 2000.

Defago, Nicki, *Child Free and Loving It!*, London, Fusion Press, 2005.

DePaulo, Bella, *Singled Out: How Singles Are Stereotyped, Stigmatized, and Ignored, and Still Live Happily Ever After,* New York, St. Martin's Press, 2006.

Douglas, Susan J. and Michaels, Meredith W., *The Mommy Myth: The Idealization of Motherhood and How It Has Undermined All Women,* New York, The Free Press, 2004.

Ehrenreich, Barbara, *Nickel and Dimed: On (Not) Getting By in America,* New York, Metropolitan/Owl Book/ Henry Holt and Company, 2001.

Fein, Ellen and Sherrie Schneider, *All the Rules: Time-Tested Secrets for Capturing the Heart of Mr. Right,* New York, Warner Books, 2007.

Gore, Al. *An Inconvenient Truth: The Planetary Emergency of Global Warming and What We Can Do about It,* Emmaus, PA, Rodale, 2006.

Giffin, Emily, *Baby Proof,* St. Martin's Griffin, 2006.

Longman, Phillip, *The Empty Cradle: How Falling Birthrates Threaten World Prosperity and What to Do About It,* New York, Perseus (Basic Books), 2004.

Orman, Suze, *Suze Orman's Insurance Kit: Evaluate Your Personal Insurance Policies On-Line Instantly!,* Hay House, 2007.

Orman, Suze, *Suze Orman's Will & Trust Kit: The Ultimate Protection Portfolio,* Hay House, 2007.

Peskowitz, Miriam, *The Truth behind the Mommy Wars: Who Decides What Makes a Good Mother?,* Emeryville, CA, Seal Press, 2005.

Shipler, David K., *The Working Poor: Invisible in America,* New York, Vintage Books (Random House), 2004.

Steiner, Leslie Morgan, *Mommy Wars: Stay-at-Home and Career Moms Face Off on Their Choices, Their Lives, Their Families,* New York, Random House, 2006.

Wattenberg, Ben J., *Fewer: How the New Demography of Depopulation Will Shape Our Future,* Chicago, Ivan R. Dee, 2004.

Weisman, Alan, *The World without Us,* St. Martin's Press, 2007.

Wilson, Edward O., *The Future of Life,* New York, Vintage Books (Random House), 2002.

Acknowledgements

My heartfelt thanks to the countless people without whom this book would not have been possible: the childfree adults who so openly shared their experiences with a virtual stranger and the friends and family who encouraged me relentlessly along the way. I appreciate you all.

Made in the USA
Charleston, SC
21 November 2010